A DORSET RIFLEMAN

BY THE SAME EDITOR

A Dorset Soldier: the Autobiography of Sergeant William Lawrence, 1790-1869
Smuggler: John Rattenbury and his Adventures in Devon, Dorset and Cornwall, 1778-1844
Costello: the True Story of a Peninsular War Rifleman
A True Soldier Gentleman: the Memoirs of Lt. John Cooke, 1791-1813

A
DORSET
RIFLEMAN

The Recollections of
Benjamin Harris

Edited by
Eileen Hathaway

Foreword by
Bernard Cornwell

SHINGLEPICKER

© Eileen Hathaway 1995, 1996
ISBN 0 9522782 2 7

First published in the UK in 1995
by Shinglepicker Publications.
Reprinted 1995.
This paperback edition
published, with an appendix, in 1996.
Reprinted 1998, 2001
Shinglepicker Publications
28 Bonfields Avenue
Swanage
Dorset BH19 1PL

British Library Cataloguing-in-Publication Data
A catalogue record for this book is available
from the British Library

Printed and bound in Great Britain
by Cox & Wyman Ltd, Reading, Berks

TABLE OF CONTENTS

ILLUSTRATIONS

Stalbridge with its 15th Century Market Cross
The castles of Cronsborg and Elsingborg, the entrance into
    the sound, with the British fleet and transport, 1807
    (Danish Expedition)
Landing of the British fleet at Mondego Bay, 1808
Attack on the French corps commanded by General Laborde,
    17 August 1808
Storming of the centre pass at Roliça
Battle of Vimeiro, 21 August 1808
Virginia Ash, Henstridge, in the parish of Stalbridge
Baker Rifles, sword bayonets, and powder horn
Private of the 95th, about 1810
Officer of the 95th, about 1811
General Robert Craufurd
Major Robert Travers
Lieutenant William Cox

MAPS

Southern England
Danish Expedition, August - October 1807
Portugal, August - October 1808
Corunna Campaign, October 1808 - January 1809
Retreat to Corunna and Vigo, 24 December 1808
    - 12 January 1809
Walcheren Expedition, July - September 1809

ACKNOWLEDGEMENTS

Collecting material for inclusion in this book took me to many locations, and I would like to thank for their help all those who work in the Public Record Office in Kew, the National Army Museum in Chelsea, Westminster City Library in Victoria, the Library and Record Office in Winchester, the Royal Green Jackets Museum also in Winchester, Folkestone and Hythe Public Libraries, and the Dorset County Record Office in Dorchester. I am particularly grateful to the staff at Swanage Library for obtaining the books I needed.

The portraits of Robert Travers and William Cox, and the photograph of the Baker Rifles, are reproduced with the kind permission of Major Cassidy of the Royal Green Jackets Museum, and with the help of their photographer Andrew Sollars. Major Cassidy has also allowed me to quote in full the text of the 95th recruitment poster of 1808, which is also on display there. The National Army Museum is the source of the illustrations of the Danish Expedition of 1807, the landing of the British army in Mondego Bay in 1808, and the battles of Roliça and Vimeiro. They are reproduced with the courtesy of the Director. The picture of General Robert Craufurd is part of the collection of Ian Fletcher, who was also immensely helpful in answering many and various queries.

I am extremely grateful to Bernard Cornwell, not only for agreeing to write a foreword, but also for his helpful suggestions. And thank you again Margaret Lamont and John Montgomery for reading and checking the manuscript.

Synjon Books have kindly allowed me to quote extracts from their version of Rifleman William Green's memoir, which was published in 1975 as *Where Duty Calls Me*. It is still available.

Last, but by no means least, I would like to thank Dawn Waring, whose wonderful portrait of Rifleman Harris so vividly and effectively encapsulates the subject, and the content, of this book.

FOREWORD

by

BERNARD CORNWELL
Author of *Sharpe's Eagle*, etc

Tall men, Rifleman Harris once observed, bore the hardships of war much less well than the short fellows, and there go my fictional heroes, Sharpe and Harper, both over six feet tall; more proof, if ever it was needed, that there is nothing like a dose of the real thing to cut fiction writers down to size. And in the memoirs of Rifleman Harris we have something very real indeed. Harris, a Dorset boy turned Rifleman, fought at Copenhagen, in Flanders and, most memorably, in Wellington's great Peninsular Campaign against the French.

Benjamin Harris must have been a Recruiting Officer's dream. Not all Britain's soldiers were rogues, drunks and felons, but certainly a high proportion of the ranks were less than model citizens, yet Harris was a fit and healthy country boy; intelligent, patriotic and, need it be said, short of stature. He had no schooling, but he brought to his memoirs a piercing eye, a talent for description, and a constant good humour.

He needed that humour for he endured some of the worst campaigns of the Napoleonic wars; notably, in Harris's case, the retreat to Corunna. Imagine a walk on broken (or no) shoes across two hundred and twenty miles of mountainous country through an early winter that brought sleet, cold and pelting rain to the Galician mountains. The men had no tents, food was usually short and always rotten, and if that was not enough, the French were on their tail with a larger and better equipped army. Maybe better equipped, but not better. Harris would never allow that. He believed he belonged to the best army in the world, and to the best regiment in that army, and to the best battalion of that regiment which, coincidentally, was commanded by the finest officers in the world who, naturally, led the best soldiers. I doubt Harris ever believed the Rifles could be beaten, nor were they, and perhaps nor could they be so long as they had men like Harris in their ranks. They were not all such fine men. Harris, at Copenhagen, threatens to shoot his front rank man (a tall man, Harris notes) for displaying cowardice, though he is quick to add that it was 'the only instance I remember of a British soldier endeavouring to hold back when his comrades were going forward', which, if true, is remarkable.

Yet it had to be a remarkable army to achieve its victories. The colours of the Peninsular regiments display some of the hardest fought battles the British army fought, let alone won, though it must be said that Harris is not the best eye-witness of those battles. This is not Harris's fault; he was a Rifleman and his horizon was very limited, as would ours be if it contained a French *voltigeur* (literally 'a vaulter') trying to shoot us. Harris sees smoke, not battles, but no other soldier of the period conveys as well as Harris just what is felt like to be in that deadly smoke. He did see Wellington in battle once, and, typical of Harris, what he notes and admires is that the great general had the presence of mind to raise his hat when greeting acquaintances. And out of battle few other military writers describe so feelingly the weight of a pack, the pinch of a boot, the bite of hunger, nor the small everyday joys of comradeship. These are wonderful memoirs, and tempted as I am to share my favourite stories in this foreword, I shall leave all the gems to this splendid new redaction that Eileen Hathaway has produced.

Wellington is famous for having described the men of his army as 'the scum of the earth', though it should be noted that he was sorely tried at the time, those men having just stripped bare a captured French treasure convoy upon which Wellington was relying for the means to pay his campaign's expenses, but Wellington offered his 'fine fellows' far more compliments than insults for he knew, better than anyone, how they could stand fire. They stood it for him at Waterloo, though Harris was not there. His soldiering career was over and, sad to relate, his country treated him badly. They cheated him of his pension, but even that betrayal will not blight Harris's essential optimism, nor his pride in having belonged, as he did, to the best company of the best battalion of the best regiment of the best army in the world, though what Harris does not note, and maybe never realised, was that it was only the best because it contained men like himself. Fiction does not do justice to such men, but Harris, thank God, does. Enjoy!

INTRODUCTION

Benjamin Harris was a soldier who served as a private in the British Army from 1803 to 1814, first in the 66th Regiment, then in the 95th (the Rifle Regiment), and finally in the 8th Veteran Battalion. He was also a shoemaker and in about 1835, when he was working as a civilian cobbler in Richmond Street, Soho, he related his military experiences to Henry Curling, an officer on half-pay in the 52nd Regiment. The result was *Recollections of Rifleman Harris*, first published in 1848. Those recollections are the basis of this book.

Since 1848, there have been several editions of the *Recollections*, all of them faithful renditions of the 1848 text, with new introductions and a few footnotes. My edition is fundamentally different because I take the view that Harris is an historical witness, not just a military one, and as such deserves a wider readership than he has hitherto received. I have therefore created a book which can be appreciated fully at the first reading by those who do not necessarily have a grounding, or even an interest, in the Napoleonic Wars. Yet there is much here to interest those already in possession of one of the earlier editions because, having researched the subject in archives, and in the regimental literature, I am able to include a great deal of previously unpublished information. I can now confirm that the Harris of the *Recollections* (who was not identified by his Christian name in the original edition) was Rifleman *Benjamin* Harris not John Harris, as has sometimes been suggested. I have been able to clarify the account with brief historical notes about the campaigns he was involved in, and to enhance it with footnotes containing facts about him and his comrades, and with quotations from the memoirs and diaries of his contemporaries in the 95th. I have also included relevant maps and illustrations.

The research I have undertaken has also enabled me to revise and restructure the text. The chronology of the 1848 text is a nightmare for readers. For example, in the chapters dealing with the battles of Roliça and Vimeiro in 1808, there were major digressions about incidents which took place at

Hythe barracks and abroad between 1811 and 1814; and a rider to the battle Roliça was printed after the account of the battle of Vimeiro. Where possible, these discrepancies have been tidied up, usually by lifting out the offending section and transferring it to a more sensible location. I have also deleted, or amalgamated, repetitious sentences and paragraphs. As a consequence, the narrative is much tighter. However, none of the facts Harris related have been edited out, and nothing has been added to his text. Additional information is presented in a way which clearly distinguishes it as such.

Although Harris' *Recollections* were first published in 1848, evidence in the text suggests that they were told to Curling at least ten years earlier. Harris tells how he encountered Robert Liston, a former comrade in the 95th, in a London street fifteen years earlier, when the two men discussed Liston's flogging ten years before that. That flogging was administered in Salamanca in late 1808 which would date the *Recollections* to about 1833. However, Harris also mentions the death of Major Robert Travers. Travers died in 1834.

A number of Peninsular War memoirs have been published over the years, but Rifleman Harris' *Recollections* are special for several reasons. Like Harris, most private soldiers of the era were illiterate, so although they greatly outnumbered officers on campaign, they are heavily outnumbered in the accounts which have survived. Asked by Curling, perhaps for the first time, to relate everything he could remember about his military career, Harris' sense of immediacy and truthfulness is impressive. Unable to read, and therefore uninfluenced by other published accounts and histories, he had only his personal experiences to draw upon, and therefore from him we get a perspective on a soldier's life which is often absent from the sometimes sanitised memoirs of officers, who could re-write their own accounts, and who often aspired to be historians rather than chroniclers of their own human experiences.

Harris, in relating only what he himself saw or knew, or sincerely believed to be true, produced wonderful thumbnail portraits of his fellow Riflemen, the ordinary soldiers of Wellington's army. He also tells us about their wives and families: Mrs Joseph Cockayne searching the battlefield for the body of her husband, and the Pullen family's troubles on the retreat to Corunna. We experience with Harris the seductive power of recruiting parties in Ireland and southern England, the medical expertise of regimental and civilian doctors, and the appeal to living soldiers of the possessions of the dead. These are the memories which make Harris so special, and the true incidents which make his *Recollections* so compelling, as you now have an opportunity to discover for yourself.

Eileen Hathaway,
1995

CHAPTER 1

Shepherd and Recruit
1781-1806

Benjamin Harris belonged to the parish of Stalbridge in North Dorset, but he was born in Portsea, Hampshire, where the parish records of St Mary's Church reveal that Benjamin Randell Harris, the son of Robert and Elizabeth Harris, was christened on 28 October 1781. Robert Harris had married Elizabeth Randell in Stalbridge on 6 August 1780. Why was Elizabeth Harris in Portsea when her son was born? We don't know, but a strong family connection with the area is confirmed by Harris in Chapter 14.

The family returned to Stalbridge where, in January 1784, Elizabeth gave birth to a second son, Augustus Frederick. Four years later, at the age of 38, she unfortunately died and in 1795, when he was 38, Robert married again. His second wife, Anne Ellot, was two years older and bore him two more children, James and Lucy.

Stalbridge was a small market town on high ground overlooking the Blackmoor Vale. At the beginning of the 19th Century, with its outlying cottages and farms, it consisted of about 140 dwellings. The population of 900 could be separated into about 147 families, two thirds of which were involved in agriculture. In 1803, the Harris household consisted of Robert and Anne, Benjamin 21, Frederick 19, James 6, and Lucy 1. It is at this point that Benjamin begins his story:

My father was a shepherd, and from my earliest youth I was a sheep-boy. Indeed, as soon almost as I could run, I began helping him to look after the sheep on the downs of Blandford in Dorsetshire where I was born. Tending the flocks and herds under my charge and occasionally, in the long winter nights, learning the art of making shoes, I grew a hardy little chap. One fine day, in the year 1803[1], I was drawn as a soldier for the Army of Reserve. Thus, without troubling myself much about the change which was to take place in the hitherto quiet routine of my days, I was drafted into the 66th Regiment of Foot and bid good-bye to my shepherd companions[2].

I was obliged to leave my father without an assistant to collect his flocks just as he was beginning more than ever to require one. Indeed, he seemed to want tending and looking after himself, for old age and infirmity were coming on him. His hair was growing as white as the sleet of our downs, and his countenance as furrowed as the ploughed fields around. He tried hard to buy me off, and to persuade the sergeant of the 66th that I was of no use as a soldier, having maimed my right hand by breaking a forefinger when a child; but the sergeant said I was just the sort of little chap he wanted, and off he went, carrying me, and a batch of other recruits he had collected, away with him. As I had no choice in the matter it was quite as well that I did not grieve over my fate[3].

Harris was selected by ballot on 13 August 1803. On 27 August he arrived at Winchester, where he joined the 66th Regiment under the command of Lt.-Col. Arthur Benson.

The first soldiers I ever saw were those belonging to the corps in which I was enrolled a member. On arriving at Winchester, we found the whole regiment in quarters. Everything was new to me, and I was filled with astonishment at the bustling contrast I had been so suddenly called into after the tranquil and quiet of my former life.

We remained at Winchester for three months. During that time, young as I was in the profession, I was picked out to perform a piece of duty that, for many years afterwards, remained deeply impressed upon my mind. It was my first lesson in the stern duties of a soldier's life.

A private of the 70th Regiment had deserted from that corps, and had afterwards enlisted into several other regiments. I was told that sixteen different times he had received the bounty and then stolen off. Being caught at last, he was brought to trial at Portsmouth, and sentenced by general court-martial to be shot.

The 66th received a route to Portsmouth to be present on the occasion. As the execution would be a good example to us young 'uns, four lads were picked out of our corps to assist, myself being one of the number chosen. Four soldiers from three other regiments were also ordered on the firing-party, making sixteen in all.

The place of execution was Portsdown Hill, near Hilsea Barracks. The different regiments which assembled - from the Isle of Wight, Chichester, Gosport, and other places - must have composed a force of about 15,000 men. The sight was very imposing, and made a deep impression on all there. Had I possessed it, I would have given a good round sum to have been in any situation but the one in which I now found myself, and when I looked into the faces of my companions, I saw by the pallor and anxiety depicted in each countenance the reflection of my own feelings.

When all was ready, we were moved to the front and the culprit brought out. He made a short speech to the parade, acknowledging the justice of his sentence, and saying that drinking and evil company had brought the punishment upon him. He behaved firmly and well, and did not seem to flinch. After being blindfolded, he was desired to kneel down behind a coffin, which had been placed on the ground.

The drum-major of the Hilsea depot gave us an expressive glance, and we immediately commenced loading. This was done in the deepest silence. The next moment we were primed and ready. There was a dreadful pause for a few moments, then the drum-major, again looking towards us, gave the signal before agreed upon - a flourish of his cane - and we levelled and fired. We had been strictly enjoined to be steady and take good aim, and the poor fellow, pierced by several balls, fell heavily upon his back. He lay with his arms pinioned to his sides, and I observed that his hands wavered for a few moments, like the fins of a fish when in the agonies of death. The drum-major also observed the movement. Making another signal, four of our party immediately stepped up to the prostrate body. Placing the muzzles of their pieces to the head, they fired, and put him out of his misery.

The different regiments then fell back by companies, and the word was given to march past in slow time. As each company came in line with the body, they were ordered to first 'mark time', and then 'eyes left', in order that we might all observe the terrible example. We then moved onwards, and marched from the ground to our different quarters[4].

The officer in command that day was General Whitelocke[5]. It was the first time of our seeing that officer, who was afterwards brought to court-martial himself.

The 66th stopped that night about three miles from Portsdown Hill. In the morning we returned to Winchester.

Whilst in Winchester, we got a route for Ireland. Embarking at Portsmouth, we crossed over and landed at Cork, where we remained nine weeks. Being a smart figure and very active, I was put into the light company of the 66th. Together with the light corps of other regiments, we were formed into light battalions and sent off to Dublin.

Whilst in Dublin, I saw a corps of the 95th Rifles, and fell so in love with their smart, dashing appearance, that nothing would serve me till I was a Rifleman myself. Arriving at Cashel one day, I fell in with a recruiting party of that regiment, and volunteered into the second battalion.

This recruiting party, who were all Irishmen and had been sent over from England to collect men from the Irish Militia, were just about to return to England. They were the most reckless and devil-may-care set of men I ever beheld, before or since. Being joined by a sergeant of the 92nd Highlanders, and a Highland piper of the same regiment - a pair of real rollicking blades - I thought we would all go mad together. We started our journey at the Royal Oak in Cashel. Early as it was, we were all three sheets in the wind. When we paraded before the door of the Royal Oak, the landlord and landlady of the inn, who were quite as lively, came reeling forth and thrust into the fists of the sergeants two decanters of whisky for them to carry along and refresh themselves on the march. The piper struck up, the sergeants flourished their decanters, the whole route commenced a terrific yell, and we all began to dance through the town, stopping every now and then for another pull at the whisky decanters. We kept this up till we had danced, drank, shouted, and piped thirteen Irish miles from Cashel to Clonmel. I never spent a day such as I enjoyed with those fellows, and on arriving at Clonmel we were as glorious as any soldiers in all Christendom would wish to be.

After about another ten days, our sergeants had collected together a good batch of recruits, and we started for England. However, a few days before we embarked - as if we had not been bothered enough with the unruly Paddies - we were nearly pestered to death by a detachment of old Irish women. On hearing that their sons had enlisted, they came from different parts to try get them away from us. They followed us down to the water's edge and clung to their offspring. When they were dragged away, they sent forth such dismal howls and moans that it was quite distracting to hear them. The lieutenant commanding the party ordered me - the only Englishman present - to endeavour to keep them back, but it was all I could do to keep them from tearing me to pieces. I was glad to escape from their hands.

At length we got our lads safe on board and set sail for England, but no sooner were we at sea than our troubles began afresh for these hot-headed Paddies - having now nothing else to do - got up a dreadful quarrel amongst themselves. A religious row took place, the Catholics reviling the Protestants to such a degree that a general fight ensued. The poor Protestants, being fewer in number, got the worst of it. As fast as we made matters up between them, they broke out afresh and began the riot again.

From Pill, where we landed, we marched to Bristol and thence to Bath where our Irish recruits roamed about the town, staring at and admiring everything they saw, as if they had just been taken wild in the woods. They all carried immense shillelaghs in their fists, which they would not quit for a moment, seeming to think their very lives depended on possession of these bludgeons, and being ready enough to make use of them on the slightest occasion.

From Bath we marched to Andover, and when we came upon Salisbury Plain, our Irish friends got up a fresh row. At first they appeared uncommonly pleased with the scene, dispersing over the soft carpet of the Downs and commencing a series of Irish jigs, but then one of the Catholics gave a whoop, leapt into the air, and dealt his partner - a Protestant - a tremendous blow with his shillelagh, which stretched him upon the sod. It was as if he had not been able to bear the partnership of a heretic any longer. This was quite enough. The bludgeons immediately began playing away at a tremendous rate, with the poor Protestants again quickly disposed of. Then arose a cry of 'Huzza for the Wicklow boys! Huzza for the Connaught boys! Huzza for Munster! and Huzza for Ulster!' and they recommenced the fight as if they were determined to make an end of their soldiering altogether upon Salisbury Plain.

We had four officers with us, and they did their best to pacify their pugnacious recruits. One thrust himself amongst them, but was instantly knocked down for his pains. He was glad enough to escape. Only when the recruits had tired themselves did they begin to slacken in their endeavours, and to feel the effect of the blows they dealt one other. They then suffered themselves to be pacified, and the officers got them into Andover where we obtained some refreshment. But we had been there only a couple of hours when these incorrigible blackguards again commenced quarrelling. Collecting together in the streets, they created so serious a disturbance that the officers got together a body of constables, seized some of the most violent, and succeeded in thrusting them into the town jail. Their companions, collecting again, endeavoured to break open the prison gates. Baffled in this attempt, they rushed through the streets knocking down everybody they met. The drums now commenced beating up for a volunteer corps of the town which, quickly mustering, drew up in the street before the jail. They were immediately ordered to load with ball. This pacified the rioters somewhat, and when our officers persuaded them to listen to a promise of pardon, peace was at last restored.

The next day we marched for Ashford, in Kent, where I joined the 95th Rifles.

Harris joined the second battalion of the 95th on 8 August 1806. His name appears on a return held at the Public Record Office in London. It contains the names of 92 men - all militiamen or reservists - who were recruited in Ireland in August and September 1806. It was these men - or a fair proportion of them - who rioted in Andover. Six - including Benjamin Harris, John Harris and William Ponton - were from the 66th Regiment, and there was one man from the 43rd

Reserve. These seven were paid a bounty of ten guineas each. The other 85 volunteers received only seven guineas each. Among the latter were John Simmons (Wexford), Hugh Doughter (Londonderry), Patrick Mahon (Cavan), Peter Hart (City of Dublin), Timothy Cadogan (South Cork) and Richard Pullen (Monaghan or North Mayo), all of whom are later mentioned by Harris.

The proportion of Irish in the 95th at this time was as high as in other English regiments, where they constituted between a fifth and a quarter of the strength. Militiamen - who were not allowed to join a line regiment until they had served at least a year in the reserve - were preferred as recruits because they were experienced in drill and discipline. Although raised by ballot, militiamen were permanent soldiers, and well trained, and several sources confirm that they made excellent riflemen. One source is William Cox, who joined the 95th two months before Harris, and was later a lieutenant in the same company. He was with one of the 95th's recruiting parties in Ireland at the time Harris enlisted, landing at Dublin and then progressing through Cashel to Clonmel, where he spent most of the summer and where he recruited 35 men of the Tyrone and Kilkenny Militias. In his memoirs he recorded that not only did these 35 recruits make excellent soldiers, but that the greater part of them were killed at the head of a storming party at the siege of Badajoz in 1812.

Edward Costello, who joined the 95th from the Dublin Militia at the end of 1807, also testifies to the quality of such men. In 1809, his battalion was raised to one thousand strong, *"chiefly through volunteers from the Militia, our common media of supply at the time.... It is justly due to the Militia regiments to say that, in the knowledge and exercise of their military duties during the war, they were very little inferior to the troops of the line. The men who joined our battalion were in general a fine set of young fellows, and chiefly the élite of the light companies of the different provincial corps."* (Costello: *Memoirs of Edward Costello,* 1852.)

Militiamen and civilians volunteered into line regiments for a variety of reasons. Some were attracted by the prospect of adventure, but the bounty was a strong incentive. So was drink - a half a pint of spirits formed part of a soldier's daily rations. Discontented farm labourers were swept into the net, and unemployed town youths. There were also runaway apprentices, like William Lawrence who joined the 40th Regiment, and sundry shady characters, including what C.W. Oman in *Wellington's Army,* describes as 'local Lotharios' evading entanglement.

All regiments exhorted potential recruits to join them, but the 95th offered them something a little different, as one of their posters, printed in Hull in January 1808, and reproduced overleaf, demonstrates.

A regiment of riflemen was a new concept in the British army and the 95th, because its men had to undergo additional training, preferred to recruit those with previous military experience. Riflemen had been used in continental armies for some years, but apart from an experimental corps which fought briefly in North America in 1780, and a few groups of foreign riflemen, who only served overseas (usually in the West Indies), the British army had not employed them. Instead, their soldiers had been armed with muskets. Muskets were very effective when fired in volleys by a body of men into a body of men, but they were notoriously inaccurate against individuals. In the hands of trained men, rifles could be deadly accurate as the American irregulars in the War of Independence had demonstrated. To make full use of the weapon's advantages over the musket, different tactics were developed for the men who were to use it.

In January 1800, an experimental corps of British riflemen had been formed at the request of Colonel

RIFLE CORPS!

COUNTRYMEN!

LOOK, BEFORE YOU LEAP:

Half the Regiments in the Service are trying to persuade you to Enlist:

But there is ONE MORE to COME YET!!!

The 95th; or,
Rifle REGIMENT,

COMMANDED BY THE HONOURABLE

Major-General Coote Manningham,

The only Regiment of RIFLEMEN in the Service:

THINK, then, and CHOOSE, Whether you will enter into a Battalion Regiment,
or prefer being a RIFLEMAN,

The first of all Services in the British Army.

In this distinguished Service, you will carry a Rifle no heavier than a Fowling-Piece. You will knock down your Enemy at Five Hundred Yards, instead of missing him at Fifty. Your Clothing is GREEN, and needs no cleaning but a Brush. Those men who have been in a RIFLE COMPANY, can best tell you the comfort of a GREEN JACKET.

NO WHITE BELTS; NO PIPE CLAY!

On Service, your Post is always the Post of Honour, and your Quarters the best in the Army; for you have the first of every thing; and at Home you are sure of Respect - because a BRITISH RIFLEMAN always makes himself Respectable.

The RIFLE SERGEANTS are to be found any where, and have orders to Treat their Friends gallantly every where.

If you Enlist, and afterwards wish you had been a RIFLEMAN, do not say you were not asked, for you can BLAME NOBODY BUT YOURSELF.

GOD SAVE the KING! *and his Rifle Regiment!*

Coote Manningham and Lt.-Col. William Stewart, who convinced the Duke of York (commander-in-chief of the army since 1798), that an infantry battalion, consisting of light, mobile troops, trained to skirmish in small detachments in support of an army, would benefit the British war effort. To be effective as skirmishers, riflemen needed to blend into the background, so the uniform chosen for them was dark green, instead of red, and they wore no ornaments of bright metal.

On 31 March 1801, the experimental Rifle Corps became official when it was granted a letter of service. Then, in January 1803 it joined the line regiments as the 95th. Almost from the beginning the men were armed with a rifle designed by the London gunsmith, Ezekiel Baker. It was accurate up to 300 yards. Each soldier also had a sword which could be fixed as a bayonet. Troop movements were carried by means of a bugle-horn. Two of the officers who were with the 95th at its inception were Major Hamlet Wade (described by those who knew him as an extraordinary, gallant, dashing Irishman), and Captain Robert Travers. Both are later mentioned by Harris.

In November 1802, five companies of the Rifles marched to Shorncliffe in Kent for the first time, and in June 1803, in response to the fear of a French invasion, a camp was formed there under Sir John Moore. Moore devised special training for the 95th, and for the other two battalions of light infantry based there - the 43rd and the 52nd, to which Henry Curling later belonged.

So pleased was the Government with the performance of the 95th Rifles that on 6 May 1805, permission was granted for a second battalion to be raised from volunteers from the militias. It was this battalion Harris joined a year later for the usual period of seven years.

CHAPTER 2

Danish Expedition
1807

In 1804, Napoleon Bonaparte, a former General in the French Republican Army, crowned himself Emperor of France and began pursuing policies which would increase the size of his Empire. He conquered Austria in 1805, Prussia in 1806, and Russia in 1807. Spain was his ally. Britain, France's strongest rival, was the only European country to remain beyond both his control and his influence, and Nelson's defeat of the combined French and Spanish fleet at Trafalgar in October 1805 so reduced Napoleon's naval power that he was unable to launch an invasion across the Channel. As an alternative, he tried to weaken Britain with economic warfare and decreed that all Continental ports be closed to British trade. He also sought to rebuild his navy and in July 1807 the British Government, fearing that the powerful Danish fleet would fall into his hands, demanded that the Danes give them temporary possession of their ships, and control of their dockyard arsenals at Copenhagen. The Danes refused, so an expedition was organised to force their compliance.

The expedition was led by Lord Cathcart and the 95th were chosen to accompany it. Five companies of the 1st battalion and five companies of the 2nd battalion were drafted into a brigade commanded by Major-General Sir Arthur Wellesley (later the Duke of Wellington). In the regiment were four men who later published accounts of their experiences: Harris;

Jonathan Leach, then captain of Harris' company; William Surtees, the 2nd battalion's new Quartermaster; and Rifleman William Green, who was in the 1st battalion. Also present was Lt. William Cox, who kept a journal and wrote an unpublished memoir[1].

The 95th embarked at Deal on 26 July 1807. The fleet arrived off Denmark on 10 August, and anchored for about six days while negotiations were held with the Danes.

> About six months after joining the 95th, four [five] companies of the second battalion were ordered on an expedition to the hostile shore of Denmark. We embarked at Deal, and landed at a little place somewhere between Elsinor and Copenhagen. It was, I think, called Scarlet Island.

On 15 August, the British anchored off Vedbaek on Zealand, about 12 miles north of Copenhagen. The troops landed the next day in flat-bottomed boats each of which also carried a cannon.

Surtees: *"Nothing could exceed the beauty and regularity in which the different divisions of boats approached the shore, covered by some small brigs and bombs, which had orders to clear the beach by grapeshot of any of the enemy that might appear"*.

> The expedition consisted of about 30,000 men, and at the moment of our getting on shore, the whole force set up one simultaneous and tremendous cheer. It is a sound I cannot describe, but it was inspiring. This was the first time I heard the sound our men gave tongue to when they get near the enemy, though my ears later became pretty well accustomed to it.
>
> As soon as we got on shore, the Rifles, as the advance, were pushed forward in chain order through some thick woods of fir. When we had cleared these woods, we approached Copenhagen. Sentries were posted on the road and openings leading towards the

town in order to intercept all corners and prevent all supplies. We occupied these posts for about three days and nights whilst the town was being fired on by our shipping. I think this was the first time Congreve rockets were brought into play. As they rushed through the air in the dark, they looked like so many fiery serpents, which must have dismayed the besieged terribly[2].

By the 24 August, the whole army had landed. The British moved into the suburbs of Copenhagen where the 95th was involved in skirmishing among the gardens and shrubs, which left them with a few casualties. When information was received that a Danish force intended to attack the British lines from the west, Wellesley's brigade was ordered to seek it out and disperse it. This was on 26 August. The Danish force was located and fell back on Köge where an action was fought. The undisciplined Danish troops, unused to opposing regular troops, were defeated. Many were killed and wounded, and about 1,500 were taken prisoner. The British casualties were light, only about seven men in the two battalions of the 95th being listed as casualties. Wellesley's success at Köge put an end to attempts to relieve the beleaguered city of Copenhagen, on which the British now focused their attention.

When the main army came up, we advanced and got as near under the walls of the place as we could without being endangered by the fire from our own shipping. We now received orders to commence firing. I shall not easily forget the rattling of the guns. I felt so exhilarated that I could hardly keep back. I was checked by Captain Leach[3], the commander of my company, who called to me by name to keep my place.

My front-rank man was a tall fellow named Jack Johnson. On him the firing had a reverse effect for he seemed inclined to hang back. Once or twice he turned round in my face. I was a rear-rank man, and porting my piece in the excitement of the moment I swore that if he did not keep his ground, I would shoot him dead on the spot, so he found it quite as dangerous to return as to go on.

I feel sorry to record the want of courage of this man, but it gives me the opportunity of saying that during many years' arduous service, it is the only instance I remember of a British soldier endeavouring to hold back when his comrades were going forward. Lieutenant [William] Cox overheard me threaten to shoot Johnson for cowardice and mentioned it to the colonel. Others got wind of the story too and Johnson was never again held in estimation by the Rifles. Indeed, such was the contempt he was held in that he was soon afterwards removed from amongst us to a veteran battalion.

The shelling of Copenhagen began on 2 September and caused so much damage that by 5 September, when the Governor surrendered, a third of the city had been destroyed. When the fighting was over, the Danish fleet - 18 ships of the line, 16 frigates, 9 gun-brigs, and 25 gunboats - and the Danish dockyards and dockyard stores, were placed in British hands. While the transfer was being completed, the British forces occupied the local towns and villages. Detachments were sent out to scour the country for pockets of resistance, and to discover and collect caches of weapons. The men of the 95th's 2nd battalion were based in Naestved, with outposts at Lundbye, Vordingborg and Praestö.

Whilst in Denmark we led a tolerably active life. The Rifles were continually on the alert, ordered hither one day, and the order countermanded the next. When wanted in a hurry, we were placed in carts and rattled over the face of the country, in company with the dragoons of the German Legion[4], so although we did not have so much fighting to do as afterwards in the Peninsula, we had plenty of work to keep us from idleness.

Occasionally, we had some pleasant adventures among the blue-eyed Danish lasses, for the Rifles were always terrible fellows in that way. A party of us occupied a gentleman's house. The family, which were residing there, consisted of the owner of the mansion, his wife, five very handsome daughters, and their servants. On the first night we were treated with the utmost civility, although it cannot have been pleasant to have a company of foreign soldiers in the house. It was doubtless thought best to do everything possible to conciliate such guests, so on this night everything was set before us as if we were their equals, and a large party of green-jackets unceremoniously sat down to tea with the family.

One young lady presided at the urn serving out the tea whilst the others sat on each side of their father and mother chatting to us, and endeavouring to make themselves as agreeable as they could. Five beautiful girls in a drawing-room were rather awkward companions for a set of rough and ready, bold and unscrupulous Riflemen, and I cannot say I felt easy. It went well for some time, our fellows drinking their tea genteelly, but bye and bye, some of them expressed themselves dissatisfied with tea and toast, and demanded something stronger. Liquors were accordingly served to them. This was followed by more familiarity. The ice once broken, respect for the host and hostess was quickly lost as I feared would prove the case. Several of the men started pulling the young ladies about, kissing them, and proceeding to other acts of rudeness. I saw that unless I interfered matters would quickly get worse, so I jumped up and endeavoured to restore order. I upbraided the men for behaving like blackguards after the kindness we had been shown. My remonstrance had some effect, and when I added that I would immediately report to an officer the first man I saw ill-use the ladies, I succeeded in extricating them from their persecutors. The father and mother were extremely grateful to me for my interference, and I kept careful guard over the family whilst we remained in that house, which luckily was not long.

Soon after this the expedition returned to England. With others of the Rifles, I came home in the *Princess Caroline*, a Danish man-of-war. We landed at Deal, from whence we had started, and from there we marched to Hythe. There we lay until 1808.

The 2nd battalion sailed from Denmark on 21 October 1807 aboard the Danish ship the *Princess Caroline*. They landed at Deal on 16 November.

The British soldiers had not been popular in Denmark, and Wellesley had to admit that though his soldiers fought well, they behaved only 'tolerably in other respects' (Longford p.135). The memorialists of the 95th had nothing but sympathy and respect for the Danes. Leach described them as a brave, honourable and manly people, Surtees as kind-hearted, hospitable and inoffensive in the highest degree. William Cox summarised the experiences of the officers in Denmark as most pleasing:

"We lived on good terms with the natives of the country, had frequent balls, to which all the best families came, and the women are very fair and handsome, the living being good and cheap."

The Danes who were taken prisoner were sent to England where John Kincaid, another memorialist of the 95th[5], but then a lieutenant in the North York militia, was one of their guards on board the *Irresistible*. The old ship was:

"laden with about 800 heavy Danes who had been found guilty of defending their property against their invaders [ie the British] and I can answer for it that they were made as miserable as any body of men detected in such a heinous crime had a right to be, for of all diabolical constructions in the shape of prisons, the hulks claim by right a pre-eminence".

Not all of the 95th served in Denmark; some companies were in South America. In October 1806, three companies of the 2nd battalion had sailed as reinforcements for a small expedition of 1600 men, commanded by William Carr Beresford, which had taken Buenos Aires from the Spanish three months earlier. Unfortunately, by the time the reinforcements arrived, Buenos Aires was back in Spanish hands, Beresford's men having been overwhelmed and imprisoned. Montevideo was successfully stormed as a preliminary to the recapture of Buenos Aires, for which further reinforcements were required. These included five companies of the 1st battalion of the 95th which arrived at Montevideo at the end of May 1807 under the command of the tempestuous General Robert Craufurd (1764-1812).

In command of the British forces in South America was Lieutenant-General John Whitelocke (1757-1833), who had taken over from Sir Samuel Auchmuty (1756-1822). Whitelocke had misgivings about the whole venture and on 20 June, in a letter to William Wyndham, Secretary of State for War, he questioned the wisdom of committing British troops to the subjugation of a universally hostile Spanish population half way across the world. Although the attack on Buenos Aires took place (in July 1807), it was a humiliating failure. Some of the British troops, unused to fighting in city streets, became isolated and entrapped. Craufurd wanted them to fight on, but Whitelocke decided they should not. He capitulated and by agreement with the Spanish, the British army withdrew completely from South America a few months later.

Whitelocke, made the scapegoat for what had been an ill-conceived venture urged on the British Government by private interests, was court-martialled at Chelsea on 28 January 1808. Found guilty, he was cashiered.

Harris was not among those who fought in South America therefore the comments he makes about events which occurred there are not those of a first-hand witness. However, at Hythe, he would have come to know men who had been present, and there is no reason to doubt the accuracy of his representation of the mood of those Riflemen, or the attitude of Craufurd, towards Whitelocke:

The unfortunate Buenos Aires affair is a matter of history, and I have nothing to say about it, but I remember the impression it made upon us all. General Whitelocke was at Buenos Aires, and during the confusion of that day, some riflemen received an order from the fine and chivalrous, but fiery Craufurd to shoot the traitor dead if they saw him in the battle.

Sir John Moore was present at Whitelocke's court-martial. We were at Hythe at the time, and I recollect our officers going off to appear against him. General Craufurd, General Auchmuty I think, Captain Elder of the Rifles[6], Captain Dickson[7], and one of our privates were witnesses.

So enraged was Craufurd against Whitelocke, that I heard say he strove hard to have him shot. I also heard that Whitelocke's father was at his son's trial, and cried like an infant during the proceedings. I was told that Whitelocke's sword was broken over his head. Four months afterwards, when our men took their glass, they used to give as a toast 'Success to *grey hairs*, but bad luck to *white-locks*'. Indeed that toast was drunk in all the public-houses around for many a day.

CHAPTER 3

Obidos and Roliça
August 1808

In 1807, persisting with his policy of economic warfare against Britain, Napoleon demanded that the Portuguese break off relations and impose a prohibition on British goods. They refused so on 20 October 1807, he declared war and sent against them, through Spain, a French army of 30,000 men under Marshal Soult. The Portuguese royal family, and a large number of senior army officers, fled to South America, and by December the French were occupying Lisbon. Then, in March 1808, no longer content to have Spain as an ally only, Napoleon sent 100,000 troops over the border and forced King Ferdinand VII to abdicate. On the throne instead he placed his own brother, Joseph Bonaparte. The Spanish people were outraged, but their rebellions were ruthlessly put down. Weakened and separated, the Spanish army was no deterrent to the French, but many of its soldiers, and the militiamen in the provinces, began to engage in an effective guerrilla war against them.

Resistance also developed in Portugal, and in June and July 1808 deputations arrived in Britain from both countries pleading for joint action to repel the invaders. The British Government agreed and a fleet which had assembled at Cork to sail to South America to fight against the Spanish, was ordered to sail instead to the Iberian Peninsula to fight for them. Sent to join the fleet were four companies of the 2nd battalion of the 95th under Major Robert Travers, including that of Captain

Jonathan Leach, in which both Benjamin Harris and Lt. William Cox were serving. William Cox's brother John, who had just joined the 95th, was placed in the company of Captain Hercules Pakenham, who was Sir Arthur Wellesley's brother-in-law.

When on campaign, six wives per company (100 men) were allowed to accompany their husbands. They were selected by ballot just before embarkation. Twenty-four women therefore, and perhaps as many children, would have sailed with the 2nd battalion on 19 June to the rendezvous at Cork.

For several weeks, the fleet remained in the Cove of Cork with the army on board, awaiting the arrival of their commander, Sir Arthur Wellesley. It eventually sailed on 12 July 1808, reaching Portugal at the end of the month.

The landings began at Mondego Bay on 1 August with the brigade of General Henry Fane (1778-1840), which included the 95th. They were completed by 8 August. The first skirmish in what became known as the Peninsular War, was at Obidos seven days later on 15 August, and the first major action was at Roliça two days after that.

In 1808, four companies of the second battalion, to which I belonged, were ordered to Portugal. It was there I first saw the French.

The sight of the shipping in the Downs [off Deal] when we embarked with about 20,000 men, was splendid. Those were times which the soldiers of our own more peaceable days have little conception of.

At Cork, our ships cast anchor and there we lay for something like six weeks without the expedition being disembarked. The exception was our four companies of Rifles, which were landed every day for the purpose of drill. On such occasions our merry bugles sounded over the country, and we were skirmished about in a very lively fashion, but were always embarked again at night.

At the end of six weeks our sails were given to the wind, and amidst the cheers of our comrades we sailed majestically out of the Cove of Cork for the hostile shore. We arrived safely and disembarked at Mondego Bay.

The Rifles were the first out of the vessels because we were always in the front in the advance and in the rear in the retreat. Like the Kentish men of old, we claimed the post of honour in the field. We were immediately pushed forwards up the country in advance of the main body. The climate was hot. With a burning sun above our heads, and our feet sinking at every step into the hot sand, we soon began to feel the misery of the frightful load we were condemned to march and fight under.

Leach: *"Keeping our right towards the sea, we marched several miles over an uninterrupted plain of white sand, hot enough almost to have dressed a beef-steak. The troops, having been on board ship so many weeks, were much fatigued with this their first day's march. We encamped near the village of Lavos, where the whole army assembled as soon as disembarkation was effected. Here we remained upwards of a week."*

The weight I myself toiled under was tremendous, and I often wonder at the strength I possessed that enabled me to endure it. Being a handicraft, I marched under a weight sufficient to impede the free motions of a donkey, for besides my well-filled kit there was a greatcoat rolled on its top, my blankets and camp kettle, my haversack stuffed full of leather for repairing the men's shoes, a hammer and other tools - the lapstone I took the liberty of flinging to the devil - and ship-biscuit and beef for three days[1]. I also carried my canteen filled with water, my hatchet and rifle, and a pouch containing eighty rounds of ball cartridge. Except for the beef and biscuits, these last were the best things I owned, and I always gave the enemy the benefit of them when opportunity offered[2].

The quantity of things I had on my shoulders was enough for my wants. Indeed it was more than enough, for it was sufficient to sink a little fellow of five feet seven inches into the earth[3]. I am convinced many of our infantry sank and died under the weight of their knapsacks alone. In those days, so awkwardly was the load our men bore placed upon their backs that the free motion of the body was impeded. The head was held down from the pile at the back of the neck, so the soldier was half beaten before he came to the scratch.

We marched till it was nearly dark, and then halted for the night. I was immediately posted sentinel between two hedges. A short time later General Fane came up and cautioned me to be alert.

"Remember, sentinel," he said, "we are now near an active enemy; therefore be careful here, and mind what you are about."

Next day the peasantry sent into our camp a great quantity of the good things of their country, and our men regaled themselves upon oranges, grapes, melons, and figs. We had an abundance of delicacies which many had never before tasted. Amongst other presents a live calf was presented to the Rifles, so on our entry into Portugal we feasted like a company of aldermen!

Leach: *"The Portuguese Junta, at the head of which, I believe, was the Bishop of Oporto, or of Coimbra, sent a present to our army, consisting of pigs, sheep, poultry, cart-loads of fruit, vegetables, and wine, the arrival of which at camp was highly acceptable; but the squeaking of pigs, the bleating of the sheep, the various and discordant notes of geese, ducks, fowls, and turkeys, with the diabolical groaning of the carts - the wheels of which are never greased in Portugal - created a concert of vocal and instrumental music no description could do justice to...*

About the 9th or 10th of August the army moved forward, the advance guard being formed by some squadrons of the 20th Light Dragoons and General

*Fane's brigade. Large pine woods, growing on an arid,
white, sandy soil, occasionally varied by uncultivated
heaths, with here and there a vineyard, constituted the
chief features of the country through which we passed in
our march of two or three days from the camp of Lavos to
Leiria."*

The next day we again advanced. We were in a state
of the utmost anxiety to come up with the French and
neither the heat of the burning sun, long miles, nor
heavy knapsacks were able to diminish our ardour. I
often look back with wonder at the light-hearted style,
the jollity, and reckless indifference with which men
who were destined in so short a time to fall, hurried
onwards to the field of strife. It was as though they had
no thought of anything but the love of meeting the foe
and of the excitement of the battle.

It was five or six days before the battle of Roliça and
the army was on the march and pushing on pretty fast.
The night before, the whole force had slept in the open
fields and, as far as I know (the Rifles being always in
the front), had been without any covering but the sky
for many days. We were pelting along through the
streets of a village and I was in the front. I had just
cleared the village when I saw General Hill (afterwards
Lord Hill)[4] and another officer ride up to a mansion and
give their horses to some of the soldiery to hold. At that
moment our bugles sounded the halt. There was a little
garden before the mansion, and I was standing leaning
upon my rifle by the gate, when the officer who had
entered with General Hill came to the door, and called
to me.

"Rifleman," said he, "come here."

I entered the gate, and approached him. He handed
me a dollar.

"Try if you can to get some wine, for we are devilish
thirsty here."

Taking the dollar, I made my way back to the
village. There was a wine-house, and the day being
intensely hot, the men were crowding around the door

clamouring for drink. With some difficulty therefore, I succeeded in getting a small pipkin full of wine, but the crowd was so great that I had as much trouble paying for it. Fearing the general would be impatient and might move off before I reached him, I returned as fast as I was able.

He was loosening his sword-belt as I handed him the wine. "Drink first, Rifleman," said he, so I took a good pull at the pipkin, and held it to him again. He looked at it, then told me I might drink it all up, for it appeared greasy. I swallowed the remainder and handed him back the dollar I had received from the officer.

"Keep the money," he said. "Go back to the village to try to get me another draught." He handed me a second dollar, and told me to be quick. I made my way back to the village, got another full pipkin, and returned as fast as I could. The general was pleased with my promptness and drank with great satisfaction, handing the remainder to the officer who attended him. If he later recollected it, that draught, after the toil of the morning march, was surely as sweet as any he has drunk since.

Harris was with an advance guard of four companies of the Rifles and four of the 60th Regiment when they encountered French pickets at the windmill of Brilos near the town of Obidos.

It was on the 15th August when we first came up with the French. Their skirmishers immediately commenced operations by raining a shower of balls upon us as we advanced, which we returned without delay. The first man hit was Lieutenant Bunbury. He was pierced through the head with a musket-ball and died almost immediately.

I had never heard such a tremendous noise as the firing made on this occasion, and I occasionally observed that the men on both sides of me were falling fast. Being overmatched, we retired to a rising ground, or hillock, in our rear, and formed there all round its summit, standing three deep, the front rank kneeling. In this position we remained all night, expecting every moment that the whole host would be upon us.

At daybreak we received instructions to fall back as quickly as possible upon the main body. Having done so, we lay down for a few hours' rest, before again advancing to feel for the enemy.

Lt. John Cox was also involved in the skirmish: *"On approaching the place, the enemy opened a fire of musketry from a windmill on rising ground adjoining the place, and a few shots came from the town. However, a rapid advance of the Riflemen drew the French from all points of their posts, but being rather too elevated with this our first collision with the foe, we dashed along the plain after them like young soldiers. We were soon brought up by a body of French cavalry advancing from the main force. A retrograde movement was now imperative, in which we lost an officer and a few men."*

Due to inexperience, the Riflemen had pursued the French pickets into the rear guard of a French force commanded by General Henri François Comte de Laborde. They were, with some difficulty, rescued by General Sir Brent Spencer but not before Lt. Ralph Bunbury and three riflemen were killed, the first British soldiers to die in the Peninsular War. Captain Pakenham was wounded. Describing this action the next day, Wellesley remarked that the troops had behaved 'remarkably well, but not with great prudence'. It was perhaps over-confidence in the riflemen, and the pugnacity of their officer, Major Robert Travers, which had got them into difficulties.

On the night of 15 August, the 95th bivouacked on an extensive knoll near the road along which the French had retired. At daylight they occupied the village of Obidos where they remained until the morning of 17 August. Meanwhile, Laborde's French force of 4,000 men was at Roliça, three miles from

Obidos. Wellesley had 15,500 men outnumbering Laborde by five to one. As Laborde was expecting General Loison with 5,000 reinforcements, Wellesley decided to attack before they arrived. He deployed his men on the battlefield, placing on his far left the 29th Regiment, and to their left the riflemen of the 95th. On the morning of the 17th, these riflemen were soon hotly engaged with the French skirmishers defending Laborde's position, which was on a knoll a hundred feet above a level dusty plain.

On the 17th, still in front, we again came up with the French. I remember observing the pleasing effect afforded by the sun's rays glancing upon their arms as they formed in order of battle to receive us. Moving on in extended order, under whatever cover the nature of the ground afforded, we - together with some companies of the 60th - began a sharp fire upon them. Thus commenced the battle of Roliça.

I do not pretend to give a description of this or any other battle I have been present at. All I can do is to tell the things which happened immediately around me, and that, I think, is as much as a private soldier can be expected to do.

Soon afterwards the firing commenced and we advanced pretty close upon the enemy. I took advantage of whatever cover I could find, throwing myself down behind a small bank where I lay so secure that, although the Frenchmen's bullets fell pretty thickly around, I was able to knock several over without being dislodged. Whilst lying in this spot, I fired away every round I had in my pouch.

After a sharp contest, we forced them to give ground, and, following them up, drove them from their position in the heights. We hung upon their skirts till they made another stand, and then the game began again.

In a letter written soon after the battle, and quoted by Verner, Leach said that at Roliça: *"the 60th and ourselves attacked the enemy's right and threw in so destructive a fire on their columns - such as we could get within shot of - as to make them retreat in great disorder. You cannot conceive, nor can anyone who was present on that day, the situation of ourselves and the 60th. We had to ascend first one mountain so covered with brushwood that our legs were ready to sink under us, [with] the enemy on the top of it, lying down in the heath, [keeping] up a hot and constant fire in our face. The men [were] dropping all around us. Before we could gain the summit, the French had retreated to the next hill when they again lay concealed, [keeping] up a running galling fire on us as we ascended. Having beaten them off the second hill and taken possession of it, the enemy retreated to a wood - there being a valley between us and it - and recommenced a most tremendous fire, having received a reinforcement. The action now became very severe."*

Laborde had a reserve position on heights one mile south of Roliça, and to this he had quickly withdrawn. As a consequence, one of Wellesley's columns, the 29th Regiment commanded by Colonel George Lake, made a premature advance and became fatally exposed to enemy attack. Seeing this, Wellesley changed his tactics and ordered a general advance.

At this battle, the 29th regiment received so terrible a fire, that I saw the right wing almost annihilated with their colonel sprawling amongst the rest. We had caught it pretty handsomely too for there was no cover for us, and we were rather too near. The living skirmishers were lying beside heaps of their dead, but we held our own till the battalion regiments came up.

'Fire and retire' is a very good sound, but the Rifles were not over-fond of such notes[5]. We never performed that manoeuvre unless it was made pretty plain to us that it was necessary. However, the 29th got their fairing here at this time, and the shock of that fire seemed to stagger the whole line. It made them recoil, and a little confusion appeared in the ranks. Lord Hill[4], who was near at hand, saw it and came galloping up. He put himself at the head of the regiment, and restored them to order in a moment. Pouring a regular and sharp fire upon the enemy, he galled them in return. He remained with the 29th till he brought them to the charge, and quickly sent the foe to the right-about. Under such a storm of balls as he was exposed to, few men could have conducted the business with more coolness and quietude of manner. I have never forgotten him from that day.

At the time I was remarking these matters, and loading and firing as I lay, a man near me uttered a scream of agony and made me forget the gallant conduct of General Hill. Looking from the 29th, who were on my right, to the left, I saw Sergeant [Alexander] Fraser, sitting in a doubled-up position, and swaying backwards and forwards, as though he had got a terrible pain in his bowels. He continued to make so much complaint, that I arose and went to him, for he was a crony of mine.

"Oh Harris!" said he.

I took him in my arms.

"I shall die! I shall die! The agony is so great that I cannot bear it."

It was dreadful to look upon him. Froth came from his mouth, and perspiration poured from his face. He was soon out of pain, thank Heaven, and laying him down, I returned to my place. I think that poor fellow suffered more the short time he was dying than any man I saw in the same circumstances. After the battle I was curious enough to return and look at him. I found that a musket-ball had taken him sideways and gone through both groins.

Within about half an hour after his death, I left Sergeant Fraser, during which time I had as completely forgotten him as if he had died a hundred years previously. The sight of so much bloodshed will not suffer the mind to dwell long on any particular casualty, even though it be one's dearest friend. There was no time to think either, for all was action with us Rifles at that moment. The barrel of my piece was so hot from continual firing that I could hardly bear to touch it, and I was obliged to grasp the stock beneath the iron as I continued to blaze away.

William Ponton was another crony of mine. He was a gallant fellow and, having pushed himself in front of me, was checked by one of our officers for his rashness.

"Keep back, you Ponton!" the lieutenant said to him more than once. But in action Ponton was not to be restrained by anything but a bullet, and this time he got one. Striking him in the thigh, it must have hit an artery for he died quickly[6].

The Frenchmen's balls were flying very wickedly at that moment so I crept up to Ponton and took shelter by lying behind him. Of his dead body I made a rest for my rifle. Revenging his death by the assistance of his carcass, I tried my best to hit his enemies hard.

The Rifles fought well this day. They seemed in high spirits, delighted at having driven the enemy before them, but we lost many men. About this period of the day, Joseph Cockayne[7] was by my side loading and firing very industriously. Thirsting with heat and action, he lifted his canteen to his mouth.

"Here's to you, old boy," he said.

As he took a pull at its contents, a bullet went though the canteen and, perforating his brain, killed him in a moment. Almost immediately, another man fell close to him, struck by a ball in the thigh.

We caught it severely just here, with the old iron playing its part amongst our poor fellows very merrily. I saw a man named Simmons[8] struck full in the face by a round shot. He came to the ground a headless trunk. Many large balls bounded along the ground amongst us so deliberately that we could occasionally evade them without difficulty. I could relate many more of the casualties I witnessed on this day, but the above will suffice.

The French were forced to retreat, which they did in an orderly manner, covered by their cavalry, through the little village of Zambugeira, which had been in their rear during the battle. It may have been near here that Harris witnessed the scenes he now describes.

There were two small buildings in our front. The French managed to get into them and therefore annoyed us much from that quarter. A small rise in the ground close before these houses also favoured them; and our men were handled very severely in consequence. So angry did they become that they would not stand it any longer. One skirmisher jumped up and rushed forward crying: "Over boys! Over! Over!" Instantly the whole line responded with "Over, over, over!" They ran along the grass like wildfire and dashed at the rise, fixing their sword-bayonets as they did so. The French light bobs, unable to stand the sight, turned about and fled. Having taken possession of their ground, we were soon inside the buildings.

After the battle, the house I was in was soon well filled with the wounded - both French and English - who had managed to get there for a little shelter. I stepped across to the other house to see what was going on. Here the wounded were lying just as thickly, and two or three surgeons were busily engaged giving them assistance. What struck me most forcibly was the wine butts which had either been perforated during the engagement, or otherwise broken. The red wine, having escaped most plentifully, had run down upon the earthen floor where the wounded were lying, soaking many of them in the wine with which their blood mingled.

After I left the house and had walked a few paces onwards, I saw some of the Rifles lying about and resting. Fatigued, I laid myself down amongst them. A great many of the French skirmishers - in their long white frockcoats, and with the eagle in the front of their caps - were lying dead about us, for this was one of the places from which they had greatly annoyed us.

Judging from their appearance, and from the wounded strewed around, we had returned the compliment pretty handsomely.

I lay upon my back and, resting upon my knapsack, examined the enemy in the distance. Their lines were a couple of miles off and were, I think, stationary until near sunset, when they began to vanish, beating towards Vimeiro.

Whilst I lay watching them, I observed directly opposite me a dead man whose singular appearance had not at first caught my eye. He was lying on his side amongst some burnt-up bushes. I don't know if the heat of the firing here set these bushes on fire; indeed, I can't say how they were ignited. All I do know is that this man, whom we guessed to have been French, was as completely roasted as if he had been spitted before a good kitchen fire. He was burnt quite brown, every stitch of clothing was singed off, and he was drawn all up like a dried frog.

I called the attention of one or two men near me, and we examined him, turning him about with our rifles with no little curiosity. I remember now, with some surprise, that the miserable fate of this poor fellow called from us very little sympathy, but seemed only to be a subject of mirth for we cracked many a joke upon the poor fellow's appearance[9].

After the battle, when the roll was called, some of the females came along the front of the line to inquire of the survivors whether they knew anything about their husbands. Amongst other names, I heard that of Cockayne called in a female voice. It was not replied to.

The name struck me, and I observed the poor woman who had called it. She stood sobbing before us, apparently afraid to make further inquiries about her husband. No man had answered to his name, or had any account to give of his fate. I had observed him fall whilst drinking from his canteen, but as I looked at the poor sobbing creature before me, I felt unable to tell her of his death. At length Captain Leach observed her, and called out to the company:

"Does any man here know what has happened to Cockayne? If so, let him speak out at once."

Upon this order I immediately related what I had seen, and told the manner of his death. Mrs Cockayne appeared anxious to seek the spot where her husband fell, and asked me to accompany her over the field. Notwithstanding what I had told her, she trusted she might find him alive.

"Do you think you could find the place?" said Captain Leach, upon being referred to.

I told him I was sure I could, as I had remarked many objects whilst looking for cover during the skirmishing.

"Go then," said the captain, "and show the poor woman the spot, as she seems so desirous of finding the body."

I accordingly made my way over the ground we had fought on. She followed sobbing. We soon reached the spot where her husband's body lay and I pointed it out to her.

She now discovered that all her hopes were in vain. She embraced a stiffened corpse, then rose and contemplated his disfigured face for some minutes. She took a prayer-book from her pocket, and with hands clasped and tears streaming down her cheeks, she knelt down and repeated the service for the dead over the body. When she had finished she appeared a good deal comforted, and I took the opportunity of beckoning to a pioneer I saw near with some other men. Together we dug a hole, and quickly buried the body.

Mrs Cockayne returned with me to the company to which her husband had been attached, and laid herself down upon the heath near us, amongst other females, who were in the same distressing circumstances. The sky was her canopy, and a turf her pillow, for we had no tents with us. Poor woman. I pitied her much, but if she had been a duchess she would have fared the same[10].

She was a handsome woman, and the circumstances of my having seen her husband fall, and having accompanied her to find his body, begot a sort of intimacy between us. Bereaved as she was, the company to which Cockayne had belonged was now her home, and she marched to Vimeiro with us, taking equal fortune.

The circumstances of our intimacy were singular, and during the short time we remained together an attachment grew between us What little attention I could pay her during the hardship of the march, I did. I also offered on the first opportunity to marry her, but she said she had received too great a shock on the occasion of her husband's death ever to think of another soldier. She declined my offer but thanked me for my good feeling towards her. She hovered about us during the battle of Vimeiro, then went with us to Lisbon, where she succeeded in procuring a passage to England. Such was my acquaintance with Mrs Cockayne[11].

CHAPTER 4

Vimeiro
August 1808

At Roliça Wellesley had had at his disposal over 15,000 troops although he used only a third of them in the action, suffering 487 casualties, half in the 29th. The dead included 17 riflemen; another 33 were wounded. Laborde, who had lost 700 men, retreated to Montachique.

While the battle of Roliça had been taking place, the French army of Andoche Junot was in Lisbon. The day after, he fell back to Torres Vedras where he was joined by Laborde, Loison and their armies. Also on the 18th, hearing that 4000 British reinforcements were off the coast near Vimeiro, Wellesley marched to cover their disembarkation. He reached Lourinha that same day, and Vimeiro, a small town on the Maceira River only 2½ miles from the sea, on the next. There he was able to cover the landings, which were already taking place. With the reinforcements was Lt.-Gen. Sir Harry Burrard who was to take command from Wellesley.

While Burrard and Wellesley were discussing their next moves, Junot made his, marching from Torres Vedras to surprise the British at Vimeiro. News of the French movement reached Wellesley on the night of the 20th, the same night that Harris and Captain Leach report that they were on picket duty in a large pine wood to the right, and to the front, of their brigade. According to Leach, the pickets were under the command of Major Hill of the 50th, but Harris mentions only Major Napier of the 50th. His account differs from

Leach's in other ways too, so it would appear that they were not on picket duty at the same time.

The night before the battle of Vimeiro, I was posted in a wood in the front of our army. As I peered into the thick wood around me I became aware of footsteps approaching, and challenged in a low voice. Receiving no answer, I brought my rifle to the port and bade the strangers come forward. They were Major Napier[1], then of the 50th foot, and an officer of the Rifles.

The major came close up to me, and looked hard in my face. "Be alert here sentry for I expect the enemy upon us tonight, but I know not how soon."

I was a young soldier then, and the lonely situation I was in, together with the impressive manner in which Major Napier delivered his caution, made a great impression on me.

I kept careful watch all night, listening to the slightest breeze amongst the foliage, in expectation of the sudden approach of the French. On that night they did not venture to molest us, but Joseph Jessop[2], one of my companions in the Rifles, sank and died of fatigue. At daybreak, some of our men buried him in the wood close to my post.

Early on the morning of the battle, I was relieved from picket duty and threw myself down to gain a few hours' repose before the expected engagement. So wearied was I with watching that I was hardly prostrate before I was in the sort of sound sleep that only those who have toiled in the field can know. But I was not destined to enjoy a long repose for one of our sergeants, poking me with the muzzle of his rifle, desired me to get up, as many of the men wanted their shoes repaired immediately. This was by no means an uncommon occurrence, and I would have gladly declined the job, but several of the Riflemen, who had followed the Sergeant, came round me and threw their shoes and boots at my head. I scrambled on my legs, and had to make up my mind to go to work.

I looked around to see if there was any hut or shed in which I could more conveniently exercise my craft. There was a house near at hand, on the rise of a small hill, so I gathered up several pairs of the dilapidated boots and shoes, and made for it. I entered and seated myself down in a small room. I took the tools from my haversack and prepared to work. As the boots of the captain of my company [Leach] were amongst the bad lot, and he was barefoot for want of them, I commenced with them.

I had worked for less than quarter of an hour, and had the captain's boot on my knees, when a cannon-ball - the first announcement of the coming battle - came crashing through the walls just above my head, completely covering the boot with dust and fragments of building.

An old and a young woman were also present. They were so scared by this sudden visitation that they ran about the room, making the house echo with their shrieks. They then rushed out into the open air, leaving me alone with the boots around me on the floor. Although I was more used to such sounds, I thought it was not the time to be mending boots and shoes, or the place to be mending them in, so I shook the dust from my apron, hastily replaced my tools in my haversack, gathered up the whole stock-in-trade from the floor, and followed the example of the mistress of the mansion, and of her daughter, by bolting out of the house.

When I got into the open air, I found all in a state of bustle and activity with the men were falling in, and the officers busily engaged. The moment I appeared, twenty or thirty mouths opened, calling out for their boots and shoes.

"You humbug, Harris; where's my boots?" cried one.

"Give me my shoes, you old sinner," said another.

"The captain's boots here, Harris. Instantly," cried the sergeant. "Make haste and fall into the ranks as fast as you can."

51

There was no time for ceremony so, letting go the corners of my apron, I threw down the whole lot of boots and shoes for the men to choose for themselves. The captain's were with them, the wax-ends hanging just as I had left them when the cannon-ball so unceremoniously put a stop to my work. Quickly shouldering my piece, I fell into the ranks as I was ordered.

Leach, in a letter written a few days later, and quoted by Verner, states that:

"On the night of the 20th I was on an out-picket with a Field Officer and 100 men. Nothing occurred during the night, but about seven in the morning the enemy began to appear on some hills in our front, and shortly [afterwards], some of their cavalry advanced towards the left of our army."

When Leach first saw the French he thought they were feigning an attack on the left, but then

"several immense columns made their appearance towards the right and centre to take our guns which were in the first line. The pickets being only a handful of men by way of a look-out to prevent surprise, were ordered to check the French columns by a running fire as much as possible, and to retreat firing.

"We remained in the wood until several men were killed and the shots flew like hail, when the Field Officer of the pickets ordered us to retreat precipitately as our Artillery dared not fire a shot at the French columns (which were pressing hastily on) till we fell back. We retreated down a vineyard and up another hill before we could gain the British lines, the whole time exposed to the fire of a battalion of infantry... When we reach the lines, the artillery opened with most wonderful effect. The 97th fired a volley and charged the French, on which they retired. I gathered the few of my scattered picket which I could get together and found our companies with the 50th Regiment in the thickest of it."

Just before the battle commenced in earnest, whilst the officers were busily engaged with their companies, shouting the word of command and arranging matters of moment, Captain Leach ordered a section of our men to move off, double quick, and take possession of a windmill, which was on our left. I was amongst this section, and I set off at full cry towards the mill, but Captain Leach espied me.

"You there, Harris!" he roared out to me. "Fall out of that section directly. We want you here, my man."

I wheeled out of the rank, and returned to him.

"Fall in amongst the men here, Harris," he said. "The cannon will play upon the mill like hail in a few moments; and what shall we do," he continued, laughing, "without our head shoemaker to repair our shoes?"

Just before the commencement of the battle, whilst standing enranked, I looked about me. Our lines glittered with bright arms, and the features of the men were stern as they stood with their eyes fixed unalterably upon the enemy. The proud colours of England floated over the heads of the different battalions, and the dark cannon on the rising ground were all in readiness to commence the awful work of death with a noise that would deafen the whole multitude. Altogether, the sight had a singular effect upon my feelings for, a few short months before, I had been a solitary shepherd upon the Downs of Dorsetshire[3], and had never contemplated any other sort of life than the peaceful occupation of watching the innocent sheep as they fed upon the grassy turf. It was the most imposing sight the world could produce.

Murphy, one of our corporals, seemed to have a presentiment of his fate before the battle began. This is by no means an uncommon circumstance for I have observed it once or twice since. Murphy was an active fellow, and up to this time had shown himself a good and brave soldier, but on this morning he seemed unequal to his duty. It was early on in the day and General Fane and Major Travers were standing together. The general had a spy-glass in his hand, and for some time looked anxiously at the enemy. Suddenly he gave the word to fall in, and immediately all was bustle amongst us. The Honourable Captain Pakenham spoke very sharply to Murphy, who appeared quite dejected and out of spirits. Others besides myself noticed it too. He was not ordinarily deficient in courage and the circumstance was talked of after the battle was over, for he was the first man shot that day[4].

As the battle had commenced, Wellesley, realising that the French were threatening to turn his left flank, redeployed his whole army about Vimeiro and reinforced the left. Knowing that the French would deploy skirmishers to fluster and confuse his infantry, he placed at the bottom of Vimeiro hill his own skirmishers, armed with rifles, to combat them. The main body of the infantry waited behind the crest of the hill, and drawn up in front of them were twelve guns. The French had seven. Wellesley had nearly 19,000 men.

It was on the 21st August that we commenced fighting the battle of Vimeiro. It was a fine bright day and, as they came on, the sun played on the arms of the enemy's battalions as if they had been tipped with gold. The French came down upon us in a column. The Riflemen immediately commenced a sharp fire upon them from whatever cover they could get shelter behind, whilst our cannon played upon them from our rear.

The first cannon-shot I saw fired missed. We all looked anxiously to see the effect of this shot, but the artilleryman had made a sad bungle, and the ball went wide of the mark. Another of the gunners - a red-haired man - rushed at the fellow who had fired, and in the excitement of the moment, knocked him head over heels with his fist.

"Damn you for a fool," he said, "what sort of a shot do you call that? Let me take the gun." He fired the next shot himself. As soon as the gun was loaded, so truly did he point it at the French column on the hill-side, that we saw the fatal effect of the destructive missile by the lane it made, and the confusion it caused. Our Riflemen, who were amongst the guns, set up a tremendous shout of delight.

The battle commenced immediately and we were soon all hard at work. I saw regular lanes torn through the French ranks as they advanced. They were immediately closed up again as they marched steadily on. Whenever we saw a round shot go through the mass, we raised a shout of delight.

I myself was very soon hotly engaged. Loading and firing away I became enveloped in the smoke I created. Such was the cloud which hung about me from the continual fire of my comrades - the white vapour clinging to my very clothes - that for a few minutes I could see nothing but the red flash of my own piece. It is a great drawback of our present system of fighting that whilst in such a state, and unless some friendly breeze clears the space around, a soldier can know no more of his position, what is about to happen in his front, or what has happened - even amongst his own companions - than the dead lying around.

The hard-pressed Riflemen were several times driven in by the French.

As usual the Rifles were pretty busy in this battle. The French, in great numbers, came steadily down upon us, and we pelted upon them a shower of leaden hail. Under any cover we could find we lay, firing one moment, and jumping up and running for it the next. When we could see before us, and we observed the cannon-balls making a lane through the enemy's columns as they advanced, we cheered and shouted like madmen.

During the heat of the day, having advanced too near their force, we were rather hotly pressed by the enemy. Give and take is all fair enough, but we were getting more kicks than halfpence, as the saying is. Their balls stung us so sharply that the officer gave the word to 'fire and retire'. Doubtless, many got a leaden messenger as they did so, thus saving them the unpleasant necessity of retracing their ground.

Obeying the order, Jock Gillespie and myself wheeled about. Just as we did so, I saw Gillespie limp along as though someone had bestowed a violent kick upon his person. He continued to load, and fire, and make off with the other skirmishers, till we halted and made another stand for when once engaged, we never went further from the enemy than we could possibly help.

Whatever treatment he had received, Gillespie seemed quite affronted by it for he loaded and fired very sharply. Once or twice I asked him where he was hit, but he seemed unwilling to say. Eventually, however, he was floored from loss of blood. Unable to continue the game any longer, he confessed, and the confession gave him as much pain as the wound.

After the battle was over, I observed him endeavouring to get about, limping as badly as if one leg was a foot shorter than the other. Our men, who had got hold of the story, kept calling after him. They made all sorts of fun about his wound and poor Gillespie, who was a very sensitive man, sat down and cried with vexation like a child. I never saw him after that night. I think his wound completely disabled him, and he eventually got a discharge[5].

Brotherwood was one of the skirmishers lying next to me during a part of this day. A Leicestershire man, he was always a lively fellow, but of a rather irritable disposition. Just as the French went to the right-about, he damned them furiously and, all his bullets being gone, he grabbed a razor from his haversack, rammed it down, and fired it after them. He was afterwards killed by a cannon-ball at Vittoria. That ball killed three of the company at the same moment - Brotherwood, Lt. Hopwood and Patrick Mahone[6].

Our feeling towards the enemy on that occasion was the north side of friendly for, greatly outnumbering our skirmishers, they had been firing upon us Rifles very sharply, as though inclined to drive us off the face of the earth. That day was the first time I particularly remarked the French lights and grenadiers who were, I think, the 70th. Our men seemed to know the grenadiers well. They were fine-looking young men with tremendous moustaches, and were wearing red shoulder-knots. As they came swarming up, they rained upon us a perfect shower of balls, which we returned quite as sharply. Whenever one of them was knocked over, our men called out: "There goes another of Boney's Invincibles!"

At Vimeiro, the rectangular columns of advancing French infantry were thirty men wide and fifty-two deep. They met first with rifle fire and a cannonade, and then a double line of British infantry delivering rolling musket-fire company by company into their dense and unwieldy ranks. Being in a thin line, all of the British infantry could deploy their muskets whereas, being densely packed, many of the French infantry could not. Their columns began to disintegrate under the fierce fire, and when the English bayonets came into play, they were forced back down Vimeiro hill. Several more French columns advanced, but met with the same reception.

In the main body, immediately to our rear, were the 52nd (second battalion), the 50th, the 43rd (second battalion), and a German corps, whose number I do not remember[7], besides several other regiments. and the whole line seemed annoyed and angered at seeing the Rifles outnumbered by the Invincibles. As we fell back 'firing and retiring' - galling them handsomely as we did so - our men cried out, as if with one voice, to charge.
"Damn them!" they roared. "Charge! Charge!"

But General Fane restrained their impetuosity. He desired them to stand fast, and keep their ground. "Don't be too eager, men," he said, as coolly as if we were on a drill-parade in Old England. "I don't want you to advance just yet. Well done, 95th!" he called out, as he galloped up and down the line. "Well done 43rd, 52nd, and well done all. If I live, I'll not forget to report your conduct today. They shall hear of it in England, my lads!"

At this moment, Brotherwood rushed up to the general and presented him with the green feather he had torn out of the cap of a French light-infantry soldier he had killed. "God bless you, general!" he said, "and wear this for the sake of the 95th."

The general took the feather and stuck it in his cocked hat. The next minute he gave the word to charge, and down came the whole line through a tremendous fire of cannon and musketry. As they came up with us, we sprang to our feet, gave one hearty cheer, and charged along with them, treading over our own dead and wounded, who lay in the front. Dreadful was the slaughter as we rushed onwards.

The 50th, Major Napier's regiment, were next to us as we went, and I remarked the gallant style in which they came to the charge. They dashed upon the enemy like a torrent breaking bounds, and the French, unable even to bear the sight of them, turned and fled. At this moment I can hear the cheer of the British soldiers in the charge, and the clatter of the Frenchmen's accoutrements as they turned in an instant, and went off[8].

They fled as hard as they could run for it, the cavalry dashing upon them. I narrowly escaped being killed by our dragoons. In the confusion, I fell whilst they were charging, and the whole squadron, thundered past, just missing me as I lay amongst the dead and wounded. So tired was I, and overweighted with my knapsack and all my shoe-making implements, that for a short time I lay where I had fallen, watching the cavalry as they gained the enemy. I observed a gallant-looking officer leading them on in that charge. He was a brave fellow, and bore himself like a hero. With his sword waving in the air, he cheered the men on, and went dashing upon the enemy, hewing and slashing at them in tremendous style. As the dragoons came off after that charge, I watched for him, but saw him no more. He had fallen. What a fine fellow! His conduct made an impression upon me. I was told afterwards that he was a brother of Sir John Eustace.

Wellesley, seeing the French columns disordered, had ordered a cavalry charge against them by the 20th Light Dragoons. Unfortunately it went out of control and many of the dragoons (including their colonel) became casualties, to no good purpose[9].

During the attacks of the French columns, Sir Harry Burrard arrived on the ridge. Burrard was senior to Wellesley but allowed him to continue directing the troops. Harris witnessed the meeting.

In these days, when so much anxiety is displayed to catch even a glimpse of the figure of that great man the Duke of Wellington as he gallops along the streets of London, it is gratifying to recollect seeing him in his proper element, ie the raging and bloody field, and to have seen him to do so commonplace a thing as lift his hat to another officer on the battle-field, as I saw him do at Vimeiro.

At the time, we were generally enveloped in smoke and ire, sometimes unable to distinguish what was going on around whilst we blazed away at our opponents, but occasionally we found time to make comments upon the game we were playing. Two or three fellows near me were observing what was going on just in the rear, and I heard one man remark, "Here comes Sir Arthur and his staff," upon which I also looked back. I caught sight of him just meeting with two other officers of high rank. They all uncovered as they met, and I saw the Duke (then Sir Arthur

Wellesley) take off his hat and bow to the other two. I don't know whether some of the men had seen them before, or whether the names were picked up from an officer, but these newcomers seemed to be well known, as was the business they were talking about. It ran along the line from one to the other that Sir Hew Dalrymple and Sir Harry Burrard were about to take the command from Sir Arthur Wellesley, although at the time it was only a random guess.

The battle, which had begun at about 9.30am, drew to a close at noon, when Wellesley urged Sir Harry Burrard to pursue the defeated French and rout Junot's army. To Wellesley's disgust, Burrard thought it more prudent to wait for Sir John Moore and his reinforcements, who had just arrived off Portugal, so an order went out to the troops to stand fast.

Just at the close of the battle of Vimeiro, when the dreadful turmoil and noise of the engagement had hardly subsided, I began to look into the faces of the men close around me to see who had escaped the dangers of the hour. Four or five days back I had done the same thing at Roliça. After such a scene, one feels a sort of curiosity to know who amongst the companions endeared by good conduct, or amongst those disliked from bad character, during the hardships of the campaign, remained alive. The ranks of the Riflemen looked very thin. It seemed to me one half had gone down.

The battle was just over, the firing had ceased, and we threw ourselves down where we were standing. A Frenchman lay close beside me. Hearing him moan, I turned my attention to him. He was badly wounded and called to me for water, which I understood him to require more from his manner than his words - he pointed to his mouth. Getting up, I lifted his head, and poured some water into his mouth. He was dying fast, but he thanked me. It was in a foreign language so I did not exactly understand the words, but I could make out what he meant by the look he gave me. Whilst I was supporting his head, Mullins, of the Rifles[10], stepped up and damned me for a fool for my pains.

"Better knock out his brains, Harris," he said; "he has done us mischief enough today, I'll be bound."

Whilst I was giving the Frenchmen the water, down in front galloped Major [Robert] Travers, who had commanded the four companies of the 95th that day. He was much liked by the men of the Rifles, and deservedly beloved by all who knew him. He was a tight hand, but a soldier prefers that to a slovenly officer. During the day I had observed him more than once, apparently in the highest spirits, spurring here and there keeping the men well up. He could not have enjoyed himself more if he had been at a horse-race, or following a good pack of hounds. And now, just as busy as before the firing had ceased, here he was plunging along, riding hither and thither, digging the spurs into his horse's flanks and avoiding, with some little difficulty, the dead and dying which were strewed about.

The major was never a very good-looking man, being hard-featured and thin - a hatchet-faced man as we used to say - but he was a regular good 'un, a real English soldier, and that's better than if he had been the handsomest ladies' man in the army. But now he disclosed what I believe none of us knew before, namely that his head was bald as a coot's, and that up to the present time he had covered the nakedness of his nob with a flowing Caxon which, during the heat of the action, had somehow been dislodged and was lost.

"A guinea," he kept crying as he rode, "to any man who will find my wig!"

Notwithstanding the sight of the wounded and dead around them, the men burst into shouts of laughter, and a 'guinea to any man who will find my wig', was the saying amongst us long after the affair.

It is said that many a man who half a dozen times has escaped the broad waves of the Atlantic, has died crossing a brook. The major escaped the shot and shell of the enemy in many a hard-fought field, coming off with credit and renown, so it is somewhat singular that the Fates destined Punch and Judy to cut his thread of life: one day, as he rode through the streets of Dublin city, his horse was startled by the clatter those worthies made with their sticks in one of their domestic quarrels and, swerving to one side, that noble soldier was killed[11].

During the battle of Vimeiro, at a time when the groans and shouts, and the noise of cannon and musketry appeared almost to shake the very ground, John Lowe, who then stood before me, turned round during a pause in our exertions and addressed me:

"Harris, you humbug, I know you have got plenty of money about you because you are always staying about and picking up what you can find on the field, but I think this will be your last field-day, old boy. A good many of us will catch it today, I suspect."

"You're right, Lowe," I said. "I have got nine guineas in my pack, and if I am shot today and you yourself escape, it's quite at your service. In the meantime, if you see any symptoms of my wishing to flinch in this business, I hope you will shoot me with your own hand."

Lowe and myself survived this battle, and after it was over we sat down with our comrades and rested. Talking over various matters, Lowe told them of the conversation we had during the heat of the day. From that moment, the Rifles had a great respect for me. A man is closely observed in the field and it is indeed singular how, from his behaviour, a man loses or gains caste with his comrades[12].

The officers too are closely observed and commented upon. The men are very proud of those who are brave in the field, and who are kind and considerate to the soldiers under them. During a battle, an act of kindness done by an officer has often been the cause of his life being saved.

Whatever folks may say upon the matter, I know from experience, that in *our* army the men prefer to be officered by gentlemen, by men whose education has rendered them more kind in manners than a coarse officer who has sprung from obscure origins, and whose style is brutal and overbearing. I have noticed that men whose birth and station might have made them fastidious under hardship and toil have, in general, borne their miseries without a murmur, whilst those whose previous life would have prepared them better for the toils of war, have been the first to cry out and complain of their hard fate. Command does not suit ignorant and coarse-minded men, with tyranny being too much used in even the brief authority they have. A soldier can be driven to insubordination by the little-minded men who worry him over trifles which a gentleman would never think of tormenting him with. The moment the severity of the discipline of our army is relaxed, it is farewell to its efficiency, but it is very injurious to a whole corps for men to be tormented about trifles, as I have at times seen.

The British losses at Vimeiro were 135 men killed (including 37 of the 95th Rifles), and 534 wounded (43 Riflemen). One of the wounded was Lt. John Cox, who received a musket ball in the shoulder. The French lost 1,800 men. These included about 350 prisoners, one of whom was a wounded infantry captain whose comments were recorded by George Simmons of the 95th in his journal, which was quoted by Verner. The Frenchman said that he had been:

"sent out to skirmish against some of these in green. Grasshoppers I call them; you call them Riflemen. They were behind every bush and stone and soon made sad havoc among my men, killing all the officers of my company, and wounding myself without [us] being able to do them any injury. This drove me to distraction. In a little time the British line advanced. I was knocked down, bayoneted, and should have been put to death upon the spot if an English officer had not saved me."

CHAPTER 5

After the Battle of Vimeiro
August 1808

After the battle of Vimeiro, with the day's work over, I strolled about the field in order to see if there was anything worth picking up amongst the dead. Upon the spot where the charge had taken place, I noticed a soldier of the 43rd and a French grenadier, lying dead close together. They had apparently killed each other at the same moment, for both weapons remained in the bodies of the slain. I also saw a three-pronged silver fork. It lay by itself and had probably been dropped by some person who had been on the look-out before me.

Further on I saw a French soldier sitting against a small rise in the ground, or bank. He was wounded in the throat, and the bosom of his coat was saturated with the blood which had flowed down. He appeared very faint. By his side lay his cap, and close to that was a bundle containing a quantity of gold and silver crosses which he must have plundered from some convent or church. He looked the part of a sacrilegious thief, overtaken by Divine wrath and dying hopelessly. I kicked over his cap, which was also full of plunder, but declined taking anything from him, fearful of incurring the wrath of Heaven for the like offence. I left him and passed on.

A little further off lay an officer of the 50th regiment, whom I knew by sight[1]. He was lying on his back, quite dead. He had been plundered for his clothes were torn open. There were three bullet-holes close together in the pit of his stomach. His epaulette had been pulled from his shoulder, and beside him lay an empty pocket-book.

I moved on a few paces, then it occurred to me that the officer's shoes might serve me, my own being considerably the worse for wear, so I went back and pulled one of his shoes off. I knelt down on one knee to try it on. It was not much better than my own, but determined on the exchange I proceeded to take off its fellow. As I did so, I was startled by the sharp report of a firelock, and a bullet whistled close by my head. Starting up, I turned and looked in the direction the shot had come from. I could see no one near me in this part of the field but the dead and the dying lying thickly all around, but it was evident that some plundering scoundrel had taken a shot at me, and the fact of his doing so proclaimed him to be one of the enemy. To distinguish him amongst the bodies strewn about was impossible. Perhaps he himself was one of the wounded?

I looked to the priming of my rifle, and again turned to the dead officer of the 50th to effect the exchange of shoes. I had hardly done so when there was another shot, and a second ball whistled past me. This time I was ready. Turning quickly, I saw my man about twenty paces from me, just about to squat down behind a small mound. I took a haphazard shot at him and it knocked him over. I ran up to him. He had fallen on his face so I heaved him over on his back, bestrode his body, and drew my sword-bayonet. The precaution was unnecessary for he was even then in the agonies of death.

It was a relief to find I had not been mistaken - he was a French light-infantryman. I took it all in the way of business: he had attempted my life, and lost his own. It was the fortune of war so, stooping down, I cut with my sword the green string that sustained his calibash, and took a hearty pull to quench my thirst.

Finding he was quite dead, I proceeded to search him, turning him about in an endeavour to find the booty I felt pretty certain he had gathered from the slain. As I did so, an officer of the 60th approached, and accosted me.

"Looking for money, my lad?" said he.

"I am, sir," I answered; "but I cannot discover where this fellow has hid his hoard."

" You knocked him over in good style and deserve something for the shot. Here," - he stooped down and felt the lining of the Frenchman's coat - "this is the place these rascals generally carry their coin. Rip up the lining, and then search in his stock. I know them better than you seem to do."

Thanking the officer for his courtesy, I proceeded to cut open the lining of the jacket with my sword-bayonet and was rewarded by finding a yellow silk purse, wrapped up in an old black silk handkerchief. The purse contained several doubloons, three or four napoleons, and a few dollars. Whilst I was counting the money - although I did not then know the value of the dollars - I heard the bugle of the Rifles sound out the assembly, so I touched my cap to the officer, and returned to them.

The men were standing at ease, with the officers in front. As I approached, Major Travers, who was in command of the four companies, called me to him.

"What have you got there, sir?" he said. "Show me."

I handed him the purse expecting a reprimand for my pains, but he only laughed as he examined it. Turning, he showed it to his brother officers.

"You did that well, Harris, and I am only sorry the purse is not better filled. Fall in," he said handing it back to me, and I joined my company.

Soon afterwards, the roll being called, we were all ordered to lie down and gain a little rest after our day's work. We lay as we had stood, enranked upon the field. In a few minutes, one half of that green line, overwearied with their exertions, were asleep upon the ground they had so short a time before been fighting on.

After we had laid for some little time, I saw several men strolling about the fields so, with one or two others of the Rifles, I quietly rose and once more looked about me to see what I could pick up amongst the slain.

I had rambled some distance when I saw a French officer running towards me with all his might and being pursued by at least half a dozen horsemen. He was a tall, handsome-looking man, dressed in a blue uniform. He ran as swiftly as a wild Indian, turning and doubling like a hare. I held up my hand, and called to his pursuers not to hurt him, but when he was close beside me, one of the horseman cut him down with a desperate blow, and the next, wheeling round, leaned from his saddle and passed a sword through his body. By their dress, I judged them to be Portuguese cavalry, but I am sorry to day there was an English dragoon amongst these scoundrels. The cause of this cold-blooded piece of cruelty - whether the Frenchman was a prisoner trying to escape - I know not, because the horsemen immediately galloped off without a word of explanation.

Feeling quite disgusted with the scene I had witnessed, I returned to my comrades. Throwing myself down, I was soon as fast asleep as any there[2]. I slept for perhaps half an hour then the bugles sounded again and we all started to our feet. Soon afterwards we were marched off to form the pickets.

Towards evening I was posted upon a rising ground, amongst a clump of tall trees. There seemed to have been a sharp skirmish here, as three Frenchmen lay dead in the long grass nearby. As I threw my rifle to my shoulder and walked past them on my beat, I observed they had been plundered. The haversacks had been torn off and some of the contents were scattered about. Amongst other things, a small quantity of biscuit lay at my feet. It is very sad but war blunts the feelings, therefore the contemplation of three ghastly bodies in this lonely spot failed to make the slightest impression upon me. Even in the short time I had been engaged in the trade, the sight had become too familiar and the biscuits, which lay in my path, I regarded a blessed windfall. I stooped and gathered them up. They were sprinkled with blood so, with my bayonet, I scraped it off and ate them ravenously.

As I stood at the edge of the little plantation, and looked over to the enemy's side, I observed a large body of French cavalry drawn up. I thought them rather too near my post and therefore kept a very sharp look-out that evening. Whilst I stood beneath one of the tall trees and watched them, it commenced raining, and they were ordered to cloak up.

At this moment, General Kellerman and his trumpets returned to the French side. Soon afterwards, the pickets were withdrawn, I was relieved from my post, and marched off to join my company. I now found that a truce had been concluded, and we lay down to rest for the night.

General François de Kellerman, one of Napoleon's cavalry generals, had earlier ridden to the English side under a flag of truce. According to Leach, this happened the day after the battle. Kellerman brought a proposal from Junot for the withdrawal of French troops from Portugal. By this time, Sir Hew Dalrymple had taken over as commander-in-chief of the army in Portugal from Sir Harry Burrard, who was now second-in-command. Dalrymple agreed a 48-hour armistice with Kellerman.

Next day was devoted to the duty of burying the dead and assisting the wounded, carrying the latter off the field into a churchyard near Vimeiro. The scene in this churchyard was somewhat singular. Two long tables had been procured from a nearby house, and were placed end to end amongst the graves. Upon them were laid the men whose limbs it was found necessary to amputate. Both French and English were constantly lifted on and off these tables. As soon as the operation was performed upon one lot, they were carried off, and those in waiting hoisted up. The surgeons, with their sleeves turned up, and their hands and arms covered with blood, looked like butchers in the shambles. As I passed I saw at least twenty legs lying on the ground, many clothed in the long black gaiters then worn by the infantry of the line. The surgeons had plenty of work on hand that day. Not having time to take off the clothes of the wounded, they merely ripped the seams, turned the cloth back, and proceeded with the operation as fast as they could.

Many of the wounded, in search of assistance, came straggling into this churchyard by themselves. I saw one man, faint with loss of blood, staggering along, and turned to assist him. He was severely wounded in the head, his face being completely encrusted with the blood which had flowed during the night, and had now dried. One eyeball was knocked out of the socket, and hung down upon his cheek.

Another man, who seemed very badly hurt, had been brought into the churchyard and propped against a grave-mound. Those who carried him placed his cap close beside his head. It was filled with fragments of biscuit. As he lay, he occasionally turned his mouth towards it, got hold of a piece of biscuit, and munched it.

As I was about to leave the churchyard, Dr. Ridgeway[3], one of the surgeons, called me back. "Come and help me with this man," he said, "or I shall be all day cutting a ball out of his shoulder."

The patient's name was Doubter, an Irishman. Disliking the doctor's efforts, he writhed and twisted so much during the operation that Dr. Ridgeway performed it only with difficulty. He found it necessary to cut very deep, and at every fresh incision, Doubter made a terrible outcry.

"Oh, doctor dear, it's murthering me you are! Blood an' 'ounds! I shall die! For the love of the Lord, don't cut me to pieces!"

Doubter was not altogether wrong. He survived the operation, but died shortly afterwards from the effects of his wounds[4].

Dismissed by the doctor I gladly left the churchyard, returning to the hill where the Rifles were bivouacked. Soon afterwards Captain Leach ordered me to get my shoe-making implements from my pack, and to commence work upon the men's waist-belts, many of which had been much torn during the action. I continued to be so employed as long as there was light enough to see by, after which I lay down amongst them to rest.

That night we lay upon the hill-side. The tents were not then with us so many of the men broke boughs from the trees at hand to make a slight cover for their heads. It was so intensely cold that I could not sleep but lay with my feet drawn up, as if I had a fit of the cramp. During the night, I was more than once compelled to get up and run about in order to put warmth into my benumbed limbs.

CHAPTER 6

Lisbon to Salamanca and Sahagun September - December 1808

For a week after the battle of Vimeiro, negotiations took place between the English and French, and an agreement - the Convention of Cintra - was ratified on 31 August 1808. Under its terms, all fortresses were to be given up to the Portuguese, and the French, with their arms, artillery, baggage and private property - much of it plunder looted from the Portuguese - were to be repatriated from Lisbon to France in British ships.

While the negotiations were going on, the British army marched from Vimeiro towards Lisbon in a leisurely manner, and the French withdrew into Lisbon. Fane's brigade (with Harris) left Vimeiro on 23 August for Torres Vedras. There they remained until the 31st when they marched to Sobral.

Rifleman William Green was in one of three companies of the 1st battalion of the 95th with Sir John Moore's reinforcements, which landed near Vimeiro on 28 August, a week after the battle. Their route towards Lisbon took them over the battlefield, and Green noted that a great number of the dead remained unburied.

On 2 September the four companies of the 2nd battalion advanced from Sobral to Bucellos where they halted for over a week. On the 10th they bivouacked in the suburbs of Lisbon in a large public pleasure-ground called the Camp Grande. On 13 September, they were placed under canvas. From their camp, they could visit the capital where they had opportunities of seeing their recent opponents. Leach:

"The French infantry were encamped in the squares of the city whilst the transports were preparing for their reception... The best possible understanding existed between the soldiers of the two armies, who were to be seen drinking, carousing, shaking hands, and walking arm in arm about Lisbon."

Such good fellowship may have existed later, but Harris reveals that the initial encounters with the French troops were overlaid with hostility and suspicion. And he should know - he was one of the first British soldiers to venture into the city:

Three day's march brought us without the walls of Lisbon, where we halted. Soon after, the tents came up and we encamped.

The second day after our arrival, as I was lying in my tent, Captain Leach and Lieutenant [William] Cox entered and desired me to rise and follow them. We went towards the town, and wandered about the streets for some time. There were no other Englishmen in the town that I could see, and I believe we were the first men to enter Lisbon after the arrival of our army without its walls.

Both officers were good-looking men, and cut a dash in the streets of Lisbon in their Rifle uniform, with the pelisse hanging from one shoulder, and with the hessian-boots which were then worn. I thought we caused quite a sensation: there were glances from the windows from black-eyed lasses as we passed, and sulky scowls from the French sentinels.

We spent some little time looking about us, then the officers spied an hotel which we entered. They went upstairs, while I went into a sort of taproom below. There I found myself in the midst of a large assemblage of French soldier. Many were wounded; some had their arms hanging in scarfs, and others were bandaged about the head and face. In short, half of them appeared to carry tokens of our bullets of a few days before.

Although my appearance caused rather a sensation, they were inclined to be civil to me. Three of four rose from their seats, and with all the swagger of Frenchmen, strutted up and offered to drink with me. I was young then and full of the natural animosity against the enemy so prevalent with John Bull. I hated the French with a deadly hatred and I refused to drink with them. Showing by my discourteous manner the feelings I entertained, they turned off, with a *'Sacré!'* and *'Bah!'*. Re-seating themselves, they all commenced talking at an amazing rate, no man listening to his fellow.

I could not comprehend a word of the language they uttered, but I could make out that I was the subject of the noise around me. I had offended them, and they seemed to be working themselves up into a violent rage. There was one fellow in particular. He had an immense pair of mustachios, and his coat was loosely thrown over his shoulders, his arm being wounded and in a sling. He rose up, and attempted to harangue the company. He pointed to the pouch at my waist, which contained my bullets, then to my rifle, and then to his own wounded arm, and I began to suspect that unless I speedily removed myself from the house, I should get more than I had bargained for on entering it.

Luckily, Lieutenant Cox and Captain Leach entered in search of me. At a glance, they saw the state of affairs and instantly ordered me to quit the room, covering my retreat themselves.

"Take care not to get amongst such a party as that again, Harris," said the captain. "You do not understand their language, but I do. They meant mischief."

We progressed through various streets, buying leather and implements for mending our shoes, when the two officers again desired me to await them in the street while they entered a shop close at hand. The day was hot and there was a wine-house directly opposite me. After waiting some time, I crossed over and went in. I called for a cup of wine and again found myself in the midst of a large group of French soldiers. Once more, I was an object of curiosity and dislike. Regardless of the clamour my intrusions had again called forth, I paid for my wine and drank it.

The host seemed to understand his guests better than I did. He anticipated mischief and tried in vain to make me understand him. Suddenly, he jumped from behind his bar, seized me by the shoulder, and without ceremony thrust me into the street. There I found the two officers who, uneasy at my disappearance, had been looking anxiously for me. I excused myself by pleading the heat of the day, and an anxiety to taste the good wines of Lisbon. Together, and with our purchases, we left the town and reached the camp.

On 13 September, William Cox wrote in his journal that: *"for the first time I entered Lisbon with Capt. Leach. The French army was still in the Square and they appeared much annoyed at their recent discomfiture."*

Next morning, Captain Leach again entered my tent. He desired me to pick out from the company three good workmen to take into the town, and seek out a shoemaker's shop.

"You must get leave to work in the first shop you can find," he said. "We have a long march before us, and many of the men are without shoes to their feet."

Carrying three small sacks filled with old boots and shoes, we entered Lisbon and went into the first shoemaker's shop we saw. A master shoemaker and three men were at work there. I endeavoured to make myself understood, but they did not seem to like our intrusion. They looked very sulky, and asked us various questions, which I could not understand. The only words I could comprehend were '*Bonos Irelandos, Brutu Englisa*'[1]. Considering we had come so far to fight their battles for them, I thought this was the north side of civil, so I signed to my men who, to cut the matter short, emptied the three sacks full of boots and shoes upon the floor. Having now explained what we would be

74

at - the boots and shoes of the Rifles speaking for themselves - we seated ourselves and commenced work forthwith. In this way we were employed whilst the army lay near Lisbon. We went into work every morning, and returned to the camp every night to sleep.

After we had been there several days, our landlord's family, who were curious about us, came occasionally to take a peep. My companions were noisy, good-tempered and jolly fellows, and usually sang all the time they hammered and strapped. The mistress of the house, seeing I was the head man, came sometimes and sat down beside me as I worked. With her she brought her daughter, a very handsome dark-eyed Spanish girl with whom, as a matter of course, I fell in love. We soon became better acquainted and one evening, as I rose to leave the shop, the mother - after having sat and chattered to me, and served me with wine and other good things - made a signal for me to follow her. She had managed to pick up a little English, and I knew a few words of the Spanish language, so we could pretty well comprehend each other. She led me into their sitting-room, brought in her handsome daughter and, without more ado, offered her to me for a wife. The offer was a tempting one, but the conditions of the marriage made it impossible for me to comply, since I was to change my religion and desert my colours. The old dame proposed to conceal me effectively when the army marched, after which I was to live like a gentleman, with the handsome Maria for a wife.

It was hard to refuse such an offer with the pretty Maria endeavouring to back her mother's proposal, but I made them understand that nothing would tempt me to desert. Instead I promised that, when I returned to England, I would to try and get my discharge, and then I would return and marry Maria.

Soon after this the army marched for Spain, and the Rifles paraded in the very street where the shop I had so long worked at was situated. I saw Maria at the window. As our bugles struck up, she waved her handkerchief. I returned the salute, and in half an hour had forgotten all about her. So much for a soldier's love.

The 95th marched from Lisbon on 15 October, but they were in the city when the French troops *"marched down to the harbour with bands playing, colours flying, bayonets fixed, [and] with all the honours of war"* as Rifleman William Green described the scene. He was not the only Englishman unhappy about the terms of the Convention of Cintra, and Burrard, Dalrymple and Wellesley were summoned home to England to account for them. Sir John Moore (1761-1809) was left in command of the army in Portugal.

The French withdrew their troops from Portugal, but they still occupied Spain therefore Moore, who had an army of 35,000 men, was instructed to co-operate with the Spanish armies in a campaign against them. At the end of October, leaving some troops behind to garrison Lisbon, he marched the rest of his army north towards Salamanca. With him went Harris and Green and their respective companies. William Cox also marched, but Captain Leach, who had contracted a fever which reduced him to a skeleton, was compelled to remain in Lisbon, where he was confined to bed for so long that he took no part in what has become known as the Corunna campaign.

The terrain the army had to traverse was so difficult that Moore sent his artillery by one route and his infantry by three others. Harris and Cox were in Fane's brigade under the command of William Carr Beresford[2]. Their route took them through Sacavem, Villa Franca, Rio Major, Leiria, Pombal and Condeixa to Coimbra, which they reached on 25 October. Here they halted until 30 October, then moved on to Celerico. They reached Almeida, on the frontier between Portugal and Spain, on 11 November, and entered Salamanca on 17 November.

Our marches were now long and fatiguing. I do not know how many miles we traversed before reaching Almeida (which I was told was the last town in Portugal), but some of my companions said we had come five hundred miles since leaving Lisbon[3].

After bidding adieu to Portugal for ever - having fought and conquered, we felt elated - Spain was before us, and every man in the Rifles seemed anxious to get a rap at the French again. On and on we toiled till we reached Salamanca.

I love to remember the appearance of that army as we moved along. It was a glorious sight to see our colours spread in those fields. The men seemed invincible. Nothing, I thought, could have beaten them. Some of the fellows in the Rifles were as desperate as any who had ever toiled under the burning sun of an enemy's country, but before a few weeks were over, I witnessed hardship and toil lay hundreds of them low.

When making for the frontiers of Spain, we had lain for a few days in the passages of a convent in Portugal, and in the square of this convent there had been a punishment parade. A Highlander of the 92nd or 79th was the culprit, and the kilts were formed to witness his punishment. Some of the Rifles were watching from the convent windows when a brickbat was hurled from one of the casements. It fell at the toe of the lieutenant-colonel in command of the regiment. He was indignant, and gazing up at the window from which the brick had been thrown, caused an inquiry to be made. Although it was between the lights when the incident happened, and therefore impossible to discover who was responsible, two or three men of the Rifles were confined on suspicion. A man named Baker[4] flatly accused Robert Liston, a corporal in the second battalion of the Rifles, of the act, whereupon Liston was marched a prisoner about a hundred miles to Salamanca where we halted for eight days. Liston often complained of his hard fate at being a prisoner so long. He was tried by general court-martial and sentenced to receive eight hundred lashes.

The whole brigade turned out on the occasion. The drummers of the 9th regiment were the inflictors of the lash and Liston received the whole sentence without a murmur. He had been a good soldier, and we were all truly sorry for him. He always declared solemnly that he had no more to do with the brickbat than Marshal Beresford who commanded the brigade. In my opinion, whoever committed the act, well deserved what Liston got.

Whilst in Spain, I never saw Liston after that punishment - I suppose he remained behind in the rear, and got on in the best manner he was able - but about ten years afterwards, I was passing down Sloane Street, Chelsea, when I observed a watchman calling the hour. It struck me that I knew his face. Turning back, I stopped him and asked if he was Robert Liston, formerly a corporal in the 95th Rifles? After answering in the affirmative, the first words he spoke were:

"Oh Harris, do you remember what happened to me at Salamanca?"

"I do well," I said.

"There is no occasion for me to deny it now, and I tell you I was never guilty of the crime for which I suffered. Baker was a villain, and I believe that he was himself the culprit."

That meeting was very nearly fifteen years ago.

In command of the brigade at the time of the incident was Marshal Beresford. He was a fine-looking soldier and equal to his business. I don't think that the French army had anything to compare with our officers. There was a noble bearing in our leaders which those on the French side did not appear to have. I recollect Marshal Beresford making a speech about greatcoat buttons. Such a subject may appear trifling for a general officer to speak on, but it was a discourse some of our men much needed, for they had been in the habit of tearing off the buttons, hammering them flat, and passing them as English coin in exchange for the good wines of Spain! The Spaniards, finding they got nothing by the exchange but trumpery bits of battered lead - and the children in that country not being in the habit of playing at dumps as ours are[5] - they complained to the marshal. Halting the brigade one day, he gave them a speech upon this fraud, and promised a handsome flogging to the first man he found whose greatcoat would not keep buttoned in windy weather.

We were seven or eight days at Salamanca, during which time the shoemakers were again wanted, and I worked with my men incessantly during their short halt[6].

On 23 November, while still at Salamanca, Sir John Moore heard that one of the Spanish armies he was supposed to unite with had been defeated by the French. On 28 November, he further learned that the Spanish army of Castanos had suffered a similar fate. Undeterred, he pushed some regiments forward to cover Salamanca. This was on 1st December. They included the Rifles who occupied the village of Villaris and barricaded the streets against the French cavalry.

Moore began to give some thought to how best to get his army back to the coast should a retreat become necessary, because even with the arrival at Salamanca on 4 December of fresh troops under Sir John Hope, he had only 20,000 men. Napoleon, massing his troops around Madrid in order to invest the city, was reported to have 250,000. Thinking Napoleon would be too occupied at Madrid to spare many men for a move towards Portugal, Moore decided to threaten his communications with France by attacking Valladolid. Madrid capitulated more quickly than Moore anticipated, but he was not deflected from his plan, and on 11 December advanced on Toro and Tordesillas. That same day William Cox reported that he marched thirty miles to Zamora.

Our marches were now even more arduous. I heard the men say we accomplished fourteen leagues [about

40 miles] a day before we halted, and on them many of us were found out. The load we carried was too great and we staggered on, looking neither to the right nor the left. If a man dropped, he found it no easy matter to get up again without assistance, but few were inclined to help their comrades when their own strength was but small. It became everyone for himself. Many died of fatigue.

Strong as I was, I was nearly floored by this march. One night, we reached a town (Zamora I think), and at the entrance of the first street we came to, the sight left my eyes, my brain reeled, and I came down like a dead man. When I recovered my senses I crawled into a door I found open and there I lay for some time, too ill to rise, unregarded by the inhabitants[7].

On 13 December, learning that Soult and his army were isolated at Sahagun, Moore resolved to attack him. That same day William Cox records that they marched twenty miles up the Duoro to Toro, halting on the 14th. That same day, Brigadier-General Stewart at the head of a hundred dragoons of the 18th Hussars, surprised a French cavalry detachment at Rueda. The next day, in a cavalry action near Valladolid, fifty French dragoons were taken prisoner. Also on the 19th December, the column with Cox and Harris continued a further twenty miles to Villa Mayor. On the 20th it marched fifteen miles to Villalon, and on the 21st, 18 miles to Villada. On that day, Lt. Cox, wrote that:

These marches are very harassing owing to the severe cold with heavy snow on these extensive plains. A very brilliant cavalry action took place in front of Sahagun early this morning between the 10th and 15th Hussars under Lord Paget; the enemy had scarcely time to form outside the town when they were charged and overthrown with a loss of 2 colonels, 10 officers and 150 prisoners, besides those sabred.

22nd, marched to Sahagun where we hoped to halt for the night, but not so, being ordered on 4 or 5 miles in

(Above) *Stalbridge with its 15th Century Market Cross.*
(Below) *The castles of Cronsborg and Elsingborg, the entrance into the sound, with the British fleet and transport, 1807. (Published 1807)*

(Above) *Landing of the British fleet at Mondego Bay, 1808*
(Below) *Attack on the French corps commanded by General Laborde,
17 August 1808. (From a watercolour by Henri l'Eveque, 1812)*

Storming of the Centre pass at Roliça.
(Engraving by J T Willmore, published 1841.)

(Above) *Battle of Vimeiro, 21 August 1808. (From a watercolour by Henri L'Eveque, 1812)*
(Below) *Virginia Ash, Henstridge, in the parish of Stalbridge*

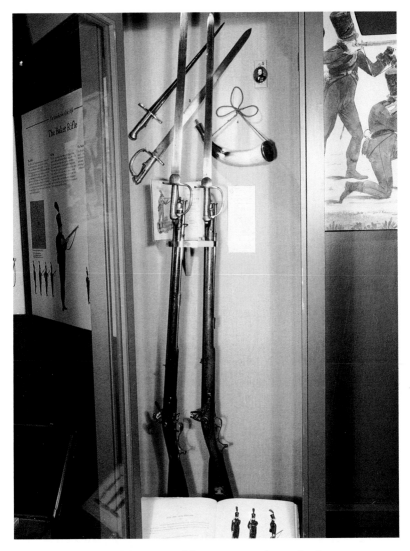

*Baker Rifles, sword bayonets, and powder horn
(Royal Green Jackets Museum).*

Private of the 95th, about 1810.
(From Goddard's 'Military Costumes of Europe', 1812)

Officer of the 95th, about 1811. (From a watercolour sketch of Captain E. Kent, made by a brother officer, and reproduced in Verner's 'History of the Rifle Brigade'.)

General Robert Craufurd

front to the monastery of Trianis where we were joined by the rest of the battalion that came out with Sir David Baird. Our march today was 17 miles through snow. Our brigade now consisted of the 1st batt. 43rd Light Infantry, 2nd batt. 52nd Light Infantry, and 2nd batt. 95th Rifle regiment commanded by Brig. R. Craufurd."

CHAPTER 7

Sahagun
December 1808

On 20 December, at Mayorga, Sir John Moore was joined by 10,000 reinforcements led by General Sir David Baird. They had marched from Corunna where they had landed on 26 October. With those reinforcements were another four companies of the 2nd battalion of the 95th, which included Quartermaster William Surtees. The two parts of the 2nd battalion (eight companies in all, consisting of 750 men) were reunited at the convent of Trianon, about two miles from Sahagun on the night of 22 December 1808, and placed in the Light Brigade under the command of Brigadier-General Robert Craufurd. The 1st battalion (which included William Green), was at full strength and was placed in the reserve commanded by Sir Edward Paget. Sir John Moore now had 25,000 men, including 2,450 cavalry and 1,287 artillerymen with 66 guns.

The four companies of the 95th, which included Harris, appear to have been almost the last of Moore's soldiers to arrive at the rendezvous at Sahagun.

> At Sahagun we fell in with the army under the command of Sir John Moore. I forget how many thousand men were there, but they were lying in and around the town when we arrived.
>
> The Rifles marched to an old convent [Trianon or Trianis] some two miles from Sahagun. There we were quartered with a part of the 15th Hussars, some of the Welsh fusiliers, and straggling bodies of men belonging

to various other regiments, who were expecting the French to fall in with them every hour.

As our small and way-worn party came to a halt before the walls of the convent, the men from these different regiments came swarming out to greet us, loudly cheering as they rushed up and seized our hands. The difference in appearance between ourselves and these newcomers was very great. They looked fresh from good quarters, and good rations. Their clothes and accoutrements were comparatively new and clean. Their cheeks were ruddy with the glow of health and strength, whilst our men were gaunt-looking and ragged, our faces burnt by the sun almost to the hue of an Asiatic's. Our accoutrements were rent and torn, and many of us were without even shoes to our feet. However, we had some work in us and were, perhaps, in better condition for it than our more fresh-looking comrades.

Nothing, I thought at that time, could tame the high spirits and thoughtlessness of the British soldier. Alas, I lived to see that I was mistaken. I saw them pretty well tamed before many more days were over our heads.

Our butchers now tucked up their sleeves, and quickly set to work, slaughtering the oxen and sheep we found within the convent walls. Our men lit fires in the open air, upon the snow, and commenced cooking the fragments, which had been cut up and distributed to them. So, very soon after our arrival, we were more sumptuously regaled than we had been for many days.

After this meal we were ordered into the convent. With knapsacks on our backs, and arms in our hands, we threw ourselves down to rest upon the floor of a long passage. Overcome with hard toil and long miles, our wearied men were soon buried in a deep and heavy sleep[1].

Quartermaster Surtees had arrived at the convent on 20 December. Harris arrived on the night on the

22nd, when he was roused from sleep by Surtees himself:

> In the middle of the night - I remember this as well as if the sounds were at this moment in my ear - my name was called out many times. I was not completely awakened by the summons, the repeated call being mixed up with some circumstance in my dreams. It was not until the noise awoke some of the men lying nearer to the entrance of the passage, and they too took up the cry, that I was effectually aroused.
>
> From weariness, and from the weight of my knapsack and the quantity of implements I carried, I was at first quite unable to gain my legs. When I did so, I found that it was Quartermaster Surtees who was thus disturbing my rest.
>
> "Come, be quick there Harris!" said he, as I picked my way by the light of the candle he held in his hand. "Look amongst the men, and rouse up all the shoemakers you have in the four companies. I have a job for them, which must be done instantly."
>
> With some little trouble, and not a few curses from them, I stirred up with the butt of my rifle several of our snoring handicrafts, and succeeded in waking them. The quartermaster bid us follow him and he led the way to the very top of the convent stairs where we passed into a ruinous-looking apartment. We walked upon the rafters, there being no flooring. He stopped when he arrived at its further extremity and called our attention to some barrels of gunpowder lying beside a large heap of raw bullocks' hides.
>
> "Now, Harris," said he, "keep your eyes open, and mind what you are about here. General Craufurd orders you to set to work instantly, and sew up every one of these barrels in the hides lying before you. You are to sew the skins with the hair outwards, and be quick about it, for the general swears that if the job is not finished in half an hour he will hang you."
>
> The latter part of this order was anything but pleasant. Whether the general ever really gave it I never

had an opportunity of ascertaining, but I give the words as they were given me. Well knowing the stuff Craufurd was made of, I received the candle from the hands of Surtees, and bidding the men get needles and waxed thread from their knapsacks, I prepared to set about the job. The quartermaster withdrew.

I often think of that night's work as I sit strapping away in my little shop in Richmond Street, Soho. It was a curious scene to look at, the task being neither very easy, nor very safe. The Riflemen were wearied, unwilling, and out of temper; and it was as much as I could do to get them to assist me. Moreover, they were so reckless that they seemed to wish to blow the convent into the air rather than get on with their work. First the candle was dropped and nearly extinguished, then they lost their implements between the rafters of the floor. They flared the light about amongst the barrels, and when I remonstrated with them, they said they wished the powder would ignite, and blow me, themselves, and the general to hell! The Riflemen of the Peninsula War were daring, reckless fellows and I had a hard task getting the work safely finished. At length, between coaxing and bullying these daredevils, I managed to do so, and together we returned down the convent stairs. Surtees was awaiting us in the passage below. He reported to General Craufurd that his order had been obeyed, after which we were permitted again to lie down, and sleep till the bugle awoke us next morning.

We remained in the convent part of the next day. Towards evening we received orders to leave all our women and baggage behind and advance towards the enemy.

On the 23 December - a cold and bitter night - the whole army was put in motion with the intention of attacking Marshal Soult, who with 17,000 men was posted behind the River Carrion.

Our four companies were quickly upon the move, and before long we came up with the remainder of the Rifle corps, which had recently arrived from England. When these men saw us coming up they halted for the moment and gave us one hearty cheer. Calling us 'the heroes of Portugal', they allowed our four companies to pass to the front as the post of honour. As we did so, we returned their cheer with pride. Our worn appearance and sunburnt look gave us the advantage over our comrades, we thought, and we marched in the van of the vanguard.

Sadly, war blunts the feelings of men and we felt eager to be at it again. As the cheer of our comrades sounded in our ears, I am afraid we longed for blood. And yet, amidst all this, even whilst they were thirsting for a sight of the enemy, softer feelings occasionally filled the breasts of those gallant fellows. As they saw the snow lying thickly in our path, some of the men near me suddenly recollected that this was Christmas Eve. It spread amongst the men. Many talked of home, and recollected previous Christmas Eves in Old England, shedding tears as they spoke of the relatives never to be seen again.

As night approached we became less talkative. The increasing weariness of our limbs kept our tongues quiet. As we walked many of us were half asleep. Then suddenly, in front, a shout arose that the French were upon us. In an instant every man was on the alert, and we rushed forward in extended order to oppose them. It proved to be a false alarm, but it nearly cost me a broken bone or two - hearing that the enemy were in sight, the honourable Captain Pakenham (now Sir Hercules Pakenham), who was mounted on a mule, made a dash to get to the front just as I was scrambling up a bank on the road side. In the darkness and hurry the mule bore me to the ground and somehow got his fore feet fixed fast between my neck and my pack, hampering us both. The captain swore, the mule floundered, and I bellowed with alarm lest the animal should dig his feet into my back, and disable me. The captain succeeded at last in getting clear and spurred over the bank. I rolled back into the road.

Unfortunately for Moore, Napoleon, learning of his advance into Spain, sent a force of about 80,000 men to find and attack him. Within hours of becoming aware of this, Moore ordered his army to retreat towards Corunna, 250 miles away. He knew that if the French reached Benevente before him, he would be cut off. It fell to the two Light Brigades (which included both battalions of the 95th), and the 7th, 10th, 15th and 18th cavalry regiments, plus a regiment of German hussars, to cover the retreat for the whole of Moore's army.

CHAPTER 8

Retreat to Corunna
24 - 31 December 1808

The retreat westward to Corunna began in the early
hours of 24 December 1808 but Harris' battalion, being
in the rear guard, did not set off until Christmas Day,
as both Lt. Cox and William Surtees confirm[1]. At the
time, even for winter, the weather was exceptionally
severe.

It must have been about 2 o'clock in the morning
that our advance into Spain was checked and the
retreat to Corunna might be said to have commenced.
General Craufurd, in command of the brigade, was
riding in front when I observed a dragoon come
spurring furiously along the road to meet us. He
delivered a letter to the general, who, the moment he
had read a few lines, turned round in his saddle and
thundered out the word to halt. A few minutes more
and we were all turned to the right-about, and were
retracing our steps of the night before. The contents of
that epistle served to furnish our men with many a
surmise during this retrograde movement.

When we again neared Sahagun, wives and
children came rushing into the ranks and embraced
the husbands and fathers they expected never to see
again. The entire Rifle corps entered the convent we
had before been quartered in [Trianon]; but this time
we remained enranked in its apartments and passages.
No man was allowed to quit his arms or to lie down, so
we dozed where we stood, leaning upon the muzzles of
our rifles.

After about an hour, we were ordered out of the convent, and the word was again given to march. There was a sort of thaw on this day, and the rain fell fast. As we passed the walls of the convent, I observed General Craufurd as he sat upon his horse watching us, and I remarked the peculiar sternness of his features. He did not like to see us going rearwards, and many of us judged by his severe look and scowling eye that there must be something wrong.

"Keep your ranks there, men!" he said, spurring his horse towards some Riflemen who were avoiding a small rivulet. "Keep your ranks and move on. No straggling from the main body."

We pushed on all the day without halting. The first thing that struck us as somewhat odd was when we passed a commissariat wagon which had been overturned and was stuck fast in the mud. It had been abandoned without an effort to save its contents. About this time, a sergeant of the 92nd Highlanders fell dead with fatigue. As we passed, no one stopped to offer him any assistance.

Night came down without - and here I speak for myself and those around me - without our having tasted food, or having halted. All night long we continued this dreadful march. Men began to look into each other's faces and ask the question: 'Are we ever to be halted again?'. Many of the weaker sort were now seen to stagger, make a few more desperate efforts, and then fall, perhaps to rise no more. Most of us had devoured all we carried in our haversacks, and endeavoured to catch up anything we could from hut or cottage on our route. Many would have straggled from the ranks and perished had not Craufurd held them together with a firm rein.

Surtees: *"On Christmas Day, our brigade, as the rear of the infantry, commenced its uncomfortable retreat, and continued marching till late at night, when we reached a convent near Mayorga. The next day, although we started early, we only reached the village of St. Miguel about midnight."*

Lt. Cox gives the march to Mayorga as being a distance of 24 miles and that to St. Miguel as being 28 miles. On the third day (27th December), they reached Castro Gonzales and Castro Pipa, two small villages within a mile of each other. It was at Castro Pipa that some of the 2nd battalion spent the night. By now the French cavalry were close on their heels.

> The enemy's cavalry were on our skirts that night, and as we rushed out of a small village - the name of which I cannot now recollect - we turned to bay. Behind broken-down carts and tumbrils, huge trunks of trees, and everything we could scrape together, the Rifles lay and blazed away at the advancing cavalry. The inhabitants - men, women and children - were aroused from their beds to behold their village almost on fire with our continued discharges. They ran from their houses crying *'Viva l'Englisa!'* and *'Viva la Franca!'* in one breath, and flew to the open country in alarm.
>
> We passed the night thus engaged, holding our own as well as we could. We were with the 43rd Light Infantry, the 52nd, a portion of the German Legion, part of the 10th Hussars, and the 15th Dragoons. Towards morning we moved down towards a small bridge. We were still followed by the enemy, whom we had sharply galled, obliging them to be more wary in their efforts.

Between Castro Gonzales and Castro Pipa was a bridge, which gave passage over the River Esla. On 28 December, the French were so close that those in Craufurd's brigade were posted in defensive positions on a height above and in front of the bridge to stall them while it was mined. Surtees: *"Our brigade was left in position to cover the working party, who were preparing to blow up the bridge, at which they worked all day."*

On this morning we remained many hours standing with our arms ported, staring the French cavalry in the face. The rain was pouring down in such torrents that the water was actually running out of the muzzles of our rifles. I did not see a single regiment of infantry amongst the French force on this day. It was a tremendous body of cavalry - some said nine or ten thousand strong - commanded, as I heard, by General Lefebvre[2].

Whilst we stood thus, face to face, the enemy horsemen sat watching us very intently as if waiting for a favourable moment to dash upon us like beasts of prey. Every now and then their trumpets would ring out a lively strain of music, as if to encourage them. The night drew on and our cavalry, moving a little to the front with several field-pieces, succeeded in crossing the bridge. We then advanced, and threw ourselves into some hilly ground on either side of the road, whilst the 43rd and 52nd lay behind a barrier they had created from some carts, trunks of trees, and other materials.

General Craufurd, standing behind this barricade, ordered the Rifles to push still further in front and conceal themselves amongst the hills on either side. A man named [Terence] Higgins was my front-rank man at this moment.

"Harris," said he, "let you and I gain the very top of the mountain and see what those French thieves are at on the other side."

My feet were sore and bleeding, and the sinews of my legs ached as if they would burst, but I resolved to accompany him. In our wearied state the task was not easy, but Higgins was tall and powerful and with his help I managed to reach the top of the mountain. There we placed ourselves in a sort of gully. Concealing ourselves by lying flat in the ditch, we looked over to the enemy's side. Thus, in such favourable situations, like cats watching for their prey, the rest of the Rifles lay upon the hills that night.

The mountain was neither steep nor precipitous on the enemy's side. On the contrary, the ascent was so easy that one or two of the videttes of the French cavalry were prowling about near where I and other Riflemen lay. We had received orders not to make more noise than we could help, and not to speak to each other except in whispers, so when one of these horsemen approached close to where I lay, I forbore to fire upon him. He stopped very near me and gazed cautiously along the ridge. He took off his helmet and wiped his face. He appeared to be meditating upon the propriety of crossing the ditch in which I lay when suddenly our eyes met. In an instant, he plucked a pistol from his holster and fired it in my face. Wheeling his horse, he plunged down the hillside. For a moment I thought I was hit, but the ball only grazed my neck. It stuck fast in my knapsack, where I found it many days afterwards while unpacking my kit on board ship.

A quarter of an hour later, I heard someone clambering up behind us. I turned quickly. It was General Craufurd, wrapped in his great-coat. For many hours the rain had been coming down furiously so, like ourselves, he was drenched to the skin. In his hand he carried a canteen full of rum and a small cup, with which he was endeavouring to refresh some of the men. He offered me a drink as he passed, and then proceeded along the ridge. After he had emptied his canteen he came past us again, and gave instructions.

"When all is ready, Riflemen," said he, "when you get the word, pass over the bridge. Be careful, and mind what you are about."

Soon after he left us we were ordered to descend the mountain-side in single file. Having gained the road, we were quickly upon the bridge. The Staff Corps had been hard at work mining the centre of the structure, which was filled with gunpowder, so we had to pass over by means of a narrow plank. All was nearly up with me. I felt that it would be all I could accomplish to reach the end of the plank, but we all got to the other side safely. Almost immediately the bridge blew up. It was a tremendous report, and a house at its extremity burst into flames. My limbs were already tremulous so the concussion of the explosion threw me to the ground where, almost insensible, I lay flat upon my face for some time. After a while I recovered, but it was only with extreme difficulty, and after many more falls, that I succeeded in regaining the column and reached Benevente[3].

Surtees was of the opinion that the mining of the bridge was a waste of time because he afterwards forded the river himself with a cartload of biscuits drawn by two bullocks. The French cavalry forded it early the following morning (29th December).

We took refuge in a convent, three parts of which was already filled with other troops: the 10th Hussars, the German Legion, and the 15th Dragoons among them. The horses were as close to them as they could be. The men were dismounted and standing between each horse, whose heads were towards the walls of the building in readiness to turn out on the instant. Liquor was handed to us by the dragoons, but we had had nothing to eat for some time so instead of receiving any benefit from it, many of our men became sick.

As soon as we arrived at the convent, every one of us was down on the floor and well nigh asleep. Half an our later we were roused from slumber by the clatter of the horses, the clash of sabres, and by men shouting to us to clear the way:

"The enemy! The enemy! Clear the way, Rifles! Up boys, and clear the way!"

The Dragoons, hardly giving us time to rise, were leading their horses amongst us. They got out of the convent as fast as they could scamper, and we were not long in following their example. That was when we discovered that the French cavalry, having found the bridge blown up, had dashed into the stream and succeeded in crossing. Our cavalry quickly formed, and charged them in gallant style.

The shock of that encounter was tremendous, and we stood enranked for some time watching the combatants. The horsemen had it all to themselves. Our Dragoons fought like tigers. Although greatly overmatched, they drove the enemy back like a torrent, forcing them again into the river. A private of the 10th Hussars - his name, I think, was Franklin - dashed into the stream after their general (Lefebvre). In the water, sword in hand, Franklin (or whatever his name was) assailed and brought him a prisoner on shore and was, I think, made a sergeant on the spot. As the French general was delivered into our custody, we heartily cheered the men of the 10th[4]. This check from our cavalry considerably damped the enemy's ardour, making them a trifle more shy of us for a while[5].

We pushed onwards on our painful march. I remember marching close beside the French general during some part of this day. He looked chapfallen and dejected as he rode along in the midst of the green-jackets.

That day's march was particularly exhausting. Cox: *"We had a most fatiguing march of about 30 miles to La Baneza, the worst I have hitherto experienced. No provisions having been issued to us at the bridge for two days, some biscuit only was obtained from carts that were too late to pass over it. No change to be had from the baggage which was far away. My last pair of shoes was torn in pieces and for the first time in my life [I was] compelled to walk barefooted for the last 20 miles over a flinty road. Up on duty all the previous night. All combined to stamp misery on the recollection."*

That same day Surtees overtook *"a most lamentable number of stragglers"* who had *"either fallen out from excessive fatigue, or from having (as in too many instances) drunk too much... The destruction of the magazine of provisions at the place we had left enabled too many of them to obtain, by one means or other, considerable quantities of spirits, which, of course, rendered them incapable of marching."*

Being constantly in rear of the main body, the scenes of distress and misery I witnessed were dreadful to contemplate, particularly amongst the women and children, who were lagging and falling behind, their husbands and fathers being in the main body in our front.

We came to the edge of a deep ravine. The descent was so steep and precipitous that in getting down it was impossible to keep our feet and we were sometimes obliged to sit and slide along on our backs. Before us rose a ridge of mountains quite as steep and difficult of ascent, but there was no pause in our exertion. Slinging our rifles round our necks, down the hill we went. The mules, with baggage on their backs, wearied and urged beyond their strength, could be seen rolling from top to bottom, many breaking their necks in the fall. The baggage, crushed and smashed, was abandoned.

As I descended this hill, I remember remarking the extraordinary sight afforded by thousands of our red-coats creeping like snails as they toiled up the ascent before us. Their muskets were slung round their necks, and they used both hands to haul themselves up. As soon as we had gained the ascent we were halted for a few minutes to give us breath for another effort, and then onwards we moved again.

I never knew exactly how many days and nights we marched, but we kept on without rest, or much in the way of food. The night brought no halt; and the long day found us still pushing on. We staggered on for about four days before we discovered the reason for this continued forced march. The discovery was made to our company by a good-tempered, jolly fellow, named Patrick McLauchlan. He inquired of our destination of an officer, marching directly in his front:

"By Jesus, Musther Hills[6]," I heard him say, "where the devil is this you're taking us to?"

"To England, McLauchlan," returned the officer, a melancholy smile upon his face, "*if we can get there.*"

"More luck and grace to you," said McLauchlan; "and it's that you're maning, is it?"

This McLauchlan was a good specimen of a thorough Irish soldier; nothing could disturb his good humour and high spirits. Even during this dreadful march, whilst he staggered under the weight of his pack, he always had some piece of Irish humour upon his tongue's end. He would have been amongst the few to reach England had he not been attacked by the racking pains of acute rheumatism. He frequently fell to the ground screaming with agony when, many times, his companions would do for him what they omitted to perform for others - halt, heave him up, and assist him forwards. Sir (then Lieutenant) Dudley Hill[6] was greatly interested for McLauchlan too, and tried to cheer him on.

The men could scarcely refrain from laughter at the extraordinary things McLauchlan gave utterance to whilst racked with pain, and staggering with fatigue. But one dark night, as we hurried through the streets of a village, McLauchlan fell, and we could not again raise him.

"It's no use, Harris," I heard him say in a faint voice, "I can do no more."

Next morning, when day broke, he was no longer seen in the ranks. As I never saw him again, I conclude he quickly perished[7].

The information McLauchlan had obtained from Lieutenant Hill quickly spread amongst us, and we saw more clearly the horrors of our situation. The men murmured at not being permitted to turn and stand at bay. They cursed the French, and swore they would rather die ten thousand deaths with their rifles in their hands in opposition, than endure the present toil.

They reach La Baneza late on the night of the 29th December. Cox: *"On arriving at La Baneza, we were put into a cold convent, the town being crowded with the*

Reserve and fatigue parties busily employed in throwing into the water ammunition which could not be forwarded... At daybreak, the Bugles sounded to march. How was I to do this with sore feet? A pair of monk's shoes was obtained without leave from a dusty corner which enabled me to get along."

On the 30 December, after a 15-mile march, they reached Zalada, about three miles in front of Astorga, and rested for the night. It may have been at Zalada that the following hasty meal was arranged.

After leaving the hills - I heard they were called the Mountains of Galicia - we passed through a village and here our major resolved to try and get a better meal than we had been able hitherto to procure. Choosing from men somewhat fresher than their comrades, he despatched a small party to try to procure something from the houses around. They purchased, shot, and bayoneted about a score of pigs, which we lugged along with us to a convent just outside the town. Halting for a short time, we proceeded to cook them, but the men were too hungry to wait for them to be properly dressed and served out.

After this hasty meal we again pushed on, still cursing the enemy for not showing themselves and allowing us to revenge ourselves on them for our present miseries.

"Why don't they come on like men, whilst we've strength left in us to fight them?" we said.

While the rear guard were in Zalada, the rest of Moore's army were in Astorga, but so too were the remnants of General Romana's defeated Spanish army. This caused serious problems because the local people preferred to give what food they had to their own troops rather than to the English. The latter, sorely tried by exhaustion and starvation, and by the knowledge that they were retreating, began looting from the houses that which was not freely given. Drink was also obtained with unfortunate consequences. There was a breakdown in discipline in some sections of the army.

It was not until the 31st that the 2nd battalion of the 95th moved into Astorga, where they halted for a few hours while the destruction of the magazine was completed. Here too the rum casks, brought by Baird's army from Corunna were staved. The contents were allowed to run in the gutters, from where some of the English troops swept it up into their caps and, to the disgust of Quartermaster Surtees, consumed it anyway.

According to William Cox, at Astorga the brigades of Craufurd and Baron Alten separated from the main army and took a route to Ponferrada via the village of Foncebadón, twenty miles away, reaching it that same night (31st December). On 1 January, they marched another twenty miles to Ponferrada where, said Lt. Cox, *"it was decided that the main body of the army should retire by Lugo on Corunna and that our brigade, with the two light battalions and the King's German Legion, should fall back by the Vigo road to secure that port, and [to] form a flanking column."*

Another reason was to lessen the strain on the resources of the commissariat. If the main objective was to keep the majority of the army safe from attack, it did not work, because the pursuing French ignored Craufurd and Alten and continued their pursuit of Moore instead.

CHAPTER 9

Retreat to Vigo
1 - 2 January 1809

Craufurd took the Vigo road, which meant he and his men would go through Orense. The army of Sir John Moore left Ponferrada for Cacabelos on the road to Corunna. In Moore's rear guard was the 1st battalion of the 95th (which included William Green). The French were close on their heels.

Surtees: *"In the morning, when we turned out to continue our march towards Orense, we heard a heavy firing towards our right and front. This proved to be an attack made by the enemy's troops on our first battalion who, with some cavalry, had been left at Cacabelos as a rear-guard."*[1]

At this time we were in the rear, following that part of the army which made for Vigo. The other portion of the British were on the main road to Corunna, and from the continued thunder of their cannon and rattle of their musketry, I judged they were closely pursued and harassed by the enemy.

It was with peculiar feelings that Craufurd seemed to sniff the sound of battle from afar. Occasionally, he would halt us for a few minutes, when the distant clamour would become more distinct. His face, turned towards the sound, would seem to light up and become less stern. Then too every poor fellow would clutch his weapon more firmly and wish for a sight of the enemy.

We were now upon the mountains. The night was bitter cold, and the snow falling fast. As day broke, I heard Lieutenant Hill say to another officer (who later sank down and died[2]):

"This is New Year's Day. If we live to see another we shall not easily forget this one."

As we proceeded, the mountains became more wild-looking and steep, and those few huts we occasionally passed seemed utterly forlorn and wretched-looking. It was a wonder how human beings could live in so desolate a home.

Being in many parts covered with ice, the hills became so slippery that our men frequently slipped and fell. Unable to rise, they gave themselves up to despair, and died. There was no longer any endeavour to assist one another after a fall; it was everyone for himself, and God for us all!

At this time, I should think that the enemy were frequently close on our trail for I heard their trumpets come down the wind as we marched[3]. Towards dusk that day I passed a man and woman lying in the snow, clasped in each other's arms. I knew them both because they belonged to the Rifles. It was Joseph Sitdown and his wife.

Poor Sitdown had not been in good health prior to the retreat, so he and his wife had been allowed to get on in front as best they could. But now they had given in, and the last we ever saw of them was on that night, lying perishing in each other's arms[4].

I never admired any man who wore the British uniform as much as I did General Craufurd. I could fill a book with descriptions of him; for I frequently had my eye upon him in the hurry of action. I like to think he did not altogether think ill of me, because he often addressed me kindly in adverse circumstances when you might have thought that he had scarcely any spirits to cheer up the men under him. The Rifles liked him but they also feared him; for he could be terrible when insubordination showed itself in the ranks.

"You think, because you are rifleman, you may do whatever you think proper," he said one day on the retreat to Corunna to the miserable and savage-looking crew around him, "but I'll teach you the difference before I have done with you."[5]

One evening, he detected two men straying away from the main body. It was in the early stage of that disastrous flight when Craufurd knew he must do his utmost to keep the division together. With a voice of thunder, he halted the brigade and ordered an immediate drum-head court-martial. Whilst this hasty trial was taking place, he dismounted from his horse and stood in the midst, looking as stern and angry as a worried bulldog.

Those nearest to him were Jagger, Dan Howard, and myself[6]. We were worn, dejected, and savage, though nothing to what we were after a few more days of the retreat. The whole brigade were in a grumbling and discontented mood. Doubtless, Craufurd also felt ill-pleased with the aspect of affairs for that man did not like retreating at all.

"Damn his eyes!" muttered Howard, and then unburdened his conscience with this growl: "It would be better if he tried to get us something to eat and drink, than to harass us in this way."

Craufurd overheard, turned sharply round, seized the rifle out of Jagger's hand, and felled Jagger to the earth with the butt-end. Jagger got up shaking his head.

"It was not I who spoke," he said. "You shouldn't knock me about."

"I heard you, sir," said Craufurd. "I will bring you to a court-martial too."

"I am the man who spoke," said Howard. "Ben Jagger never said a word."

"Very well," returned Craufurd, "then I'll try you, sir."

When the other affair was disposed of - the two men were sentenced to a hundred lashes apiece - Howard's case came on and he was promised a complement of three hundred lashes. By that time it was too dark to inflict the punishments so Craufurd gave the word to the brigade to move on. All that night he marched on foot. When the morning dawned, he looked like the rest of us, his hair, beard, and eyebrows covered with frost as if he had grown white with age. Almost immediately he called a halt. We were then on the hills[7].

Ordering a square to be formed, he ordered the three men to be brought into it. This was no time to be lax on discipline, and the general knew it for some of the men were becoming careless and ruffianly in their demeanour. He spoke to the brigade in these words:

"Although I should obtain the goodwill neither of the officers nor the men of the brigade by so doing, I am here resolved to punish these three men according to the sentence awarded, even though the French are at our heels. Begin with Daniel Howard."

There was some difficulty in finding a place to tie Howard up, as the light brigade carried no halberds. However, near at hand grew a slender ash tree and they led him to it.

"Don't trouble yourselves about tying *me* up," said Howard, folding his arms. "I'll take my punishment like a man."

And he did so without a murmur, receiving the whole three hundred. His wife - a strong, hardy Irishwoman - was with us, and when it was over she stepped up and covered Howard with his grey greatcoat. I think the general knew the enemy was too near to punish the other two delinquents just then and he gave the order to move on. We proceeded out of the cornfield in which we had been halted, and toiled away upon the hills once more. Howard's wife carried his jacket, knapsack, and pouch, which the lacerated state of his back would not permit him to bear[8].

It could not have been more than an hour after Howard's punishment that the general again gave the word for the brigade to halt. We had begun to suppose that, under the present difficulties and hardship of the retreat, he intended to allow the other two delinquents to escape, but he was not the forgetful sort when the discipline of the army under him made severity necessary; he once more formed us into square.

"Bring out the other two men of the 95th who were tried last night," he said.

The two men were brought forth. At the same time, their lieutenant-colonel, Hamlet Wade[9], stepped forward and walked up to the general. Lowering his sword, he requested that Craufurd forgive the men as they were both good soldiers and had fought in all the battles of Portugal.

"I order *you*, sir," said the general, "to do your duty. These men shall be punished."

The lieutenant-colonel recovered his sword, turned about, and fell back to the front of the Rifles. Upon this, one of the men (Armstrong I think[10]), immediately began to unstrap his knapsack and prepare for the lash. Craufurd turned about and walked up to one side of the square. Turning sharp round, he returned toward the two prisoners.

"Stop," he said. "In consequence of the intercession of your lieutenant-colonel, I will allow you this much: you shall draw lots, and the winner shall escape. But one of the two I am determined to make an example of."

The square was formed in a stubble-field, so the sergeant-major of the Rifles immediately stooped down and plucked up two straws. Coming forward, the men drew. I think it was Armstrong who drew the longest straw, and won the safety of his hide. In quick time, his fellow gamester was tied to a tree, and the punishment commenced. A hundred was the sentence, but when the bugler had counted seventy-five, the general granted him a further indulgence, and ordered him to be taken down to join his company. The general called for his horse and mounted for the first time in many hours, not having ridden since the drum-head court-martial had taken place the previous evening. But before he put the brigade in motion again, he gave us another short specimen of his eloquence:

"I give you all notice that I will halt the brigade again the very first moment I perceive any man disobeying my orders, and try him by court-martial on the spot."

He then gave us the word, and we resumed our march.

Many who read this, especially in these peaceful times, may suppose this punishment was cruel and unnecessary, given the dreadful and harassing circumstances of that retreat, but I who was there, and who was besides a common soldier of the regiment to which these men belonged, say it *was quite necessary*. No man but one formed of stuff like General Craufurd could have saved the brigade from perishing altogether, and if he flogged two, he saved hundreds from death by his management. I detest the sight of the lash, but I am convinced the British army can never go on without it. Late events have taught us the necessity of such measures[11].

CHAPTER 10

Recollections of the Retreat

It has proved so difficult to place some of Harris'
recollections of the retreat into the main sequence of
events that they have been brought together in this
chapter.

Many trivial things which happened during the
retreat to Corunna have been branded into my
remembrance. I recollect the most trifling incidents
during that march. We were, for example, joined by a
young recruit when such an addition was anything but
wished for during the disasters of the hour.

Soon after I myself put on the green jacket, a youth
by the name of Medley joined the Rifles. He was a small
chap, being under the standard by one inch[1]. He was
not rejected because our officers thought he promised
fair to become a tall fellow. He did not disappoint them:
on the day he first joined the Rifles he was five feet one
inch in height, and on the day he was killed - at
Barrossa - he was exactly six feet one.

Medley was celebrated for being the greatest
grumbler, the greatest eater, and the most quarrelsome
fellow in the whole corps, and he cut a most desperate
figure in the retreat to Corunna, where he had enough
to bear of fatigue and hunger when very little of either
could make him extremely bad company. He was such
a capital feeder that his own allowance was not half
enough to satisfy his cravings, and he often got some of
his comrades to help him out with a portion of theirs.
For about two years he was my comrade, and as I was
a shoemaker, I often had food to give him. Indeed it

was necessary to do so, or find some provision elsewhere, for he could be the most cross-grained fellow if his belly was not filled. It was dangerous sometimes to bid him hold his tongue, for he had picked up since he was five feet one, and had grown bony as well as tall. He would challenge - and could thrash - any man in the corps.

Corunna took the desire for boxing quite out of him, but it could not stop his growling, and he sprawled, scrambled and swore his way through that business somehow. If General Craufurd could have heard but a twentieth of what I heard Medley utter about him on that retreat, he would have cut Medley in half.

He carried his ill-humour with him to the very last hour of his life. Knocked over at Barrossa by a musket-ball in the thigh, he was spoken to as he lay by some of his comrades. They asked if they should assist, and carry him to the rear, but he bid them to mind their own business.

"Go, and be damned!" he said, and abused them till they passed on.

I was told this by the very men who had spoken to him, and who got his blessing as he lay[2].

In the retreat, we had another tall fellow in the four companies of Rifles. His name was Terence Higgins[3]. He was six feet one and a half, and quite as lank and bony as Medley. He was an ill-tempered fellow too, but nothing to compare with Medley either in eating or grumbling. Tall men seemed to bear fatigue much worse than the short ones, and Higgins, amongst other big 'uns, was dreadfully put to it to keep on. Half way through the business we lost him entirely. During a short halt of about ten minutes, he was reprimanded by one of our officers for the slovenly state of his clothing and accoutrements, for his dress was almost dropping from his lower limbs, and his knapsack was hanging by a strap or two down about his waist. Higgins did not take at all kindly to being quarrelled with at such a time. Uttering sundry impertinences, he desired to know if they were ever to be allowed to halt any more, and added that he did not see how he was to be very smart after what he had gone through.

Upon hearing this, the officer spoke to one of the sergeants and bid him remember that, if they got to their journey's end, Higgins was to have an extra guard for his behaviour.

"Oh!" says Higgins, "then damn me if I ever take it!" and as we all moved on at the word to march, he turned about and marched off in the contrary direction. From that hour, we never saw nor heard of him, and it was supposed that he either perished alone in the night, or joined the French, who were at our heels[4].

These, the two tallest men in the four companies of Rifles, were both in the company I belonged to, Higgins being the right-hand man, and Medley the left-hand.

During the retreat, one of the men's wives was struggling forward in the ranks with us. She presented a ghastly picture of illness, misery, and fatigue, being very large in the family way. Towards evening she stepped from amongst the crowd and lay herself down amidst the snow, just off the main road. The enemy were not far behind and the night was coming down. Her husband remained with her, and I heard one or two hasty observations from our men that the two had taken possession of their last resting-place, for to remain behind the column of march in such weather was to perish. We soon forgot about them, but a little time afterwards, to my surprise (I then being in the rear of our party), I saw the woman and her husband hurrying after us. In her arms she carried the babe she had just given birth to. Between them they managed to carry that infant to the end of the retreat, where we embarked.

The woman's name was McGuire, and luckily for her and her babe, she was a sturdy and hardy Irishwoman, for that night the cold and sleet were sufficient to try the constitution of most females. When darkness came on I lost sight of her, but with the dawn I noted with some surprise that she was still amongst us. It is said that God tempers the wind to the shorn lamb - that boy I saw many years afterwards when he was a strong and healthy lad[5].

As a result of foul roads and long miles, most of our shoes and boots were either destroyed or useless to us. Many of the men were entirely barefooted, and our knapsacks and accoutrements were in a dilapidated state. The plight of most of our officers was equally miserable. They were pallid and way-worn, their feet were bleeding, and their faces overgrown with beards of many days' growth[6].

Some of the men became careless and ruffianly in their demeanour; others I saw with tears falling down their cheeks from the agony of their bleeding feet. Many were ill with dysentery from the effects of the bad food they got hold of and had devoured on the road. On this prolonged march, our knapsacks were also our enemy. I am convinced that many a man who would have borne up well to the end of the retreat, died because of the infernal load he carried on his back. My own knapsack was my bitterest enemy, and I felt I would die in its deadly embrace. The knapsacks should have been abandoned at the very commencement of the retrograde movement for it would have been better to lose them instead of the poor fellows who died on the road strapped to them[7].

What a contrast our corps displayed to how I remembered them on that morning in Ireland when their dashing appearance captivated my fancy! Now many of the poor fellows, nearly sinking with fatigue, reeled as if in a state of drunkenness. We looked like ghosts of our former selves, but we held on resolutely and our officers behaved most nobly. Craufurd was not to be daunted by long miles, fatigue, or fine weather, and many a man in that retreat caught courage from his stern eye and gallant bearing. I don't think the world ever saw a more perfect soldier than General Craufurd.

I remember one night, we halted for a couple of hours in a small village. With several others I sought shelter at the first roof I saw, which was the stable of a sort of farm-house. Here we found nothing in the way of food but some raw potatoes, which were lying in a heap in one of the empty stalls. For want of better rations, we made a meal of them then threw ourselves down upon the stones with which the place was paved. Some of our other men, together with two or three of our officers, were more fortunate, having possession of the rooms of the adjoining building, where they at least found a fire to warm themselves.

One of the officers was Lieutenant Hill, and with him on this retreat was his black servant, a youth he had brought with him from Montevideo where, I heard, the Rifles had found him tied to a gun they had captured[8]. This lad came to where I lay in the mule-stable and aroused me. He desired me to speak with his master in the adjoining room, which I entered. I found the lieutenant seated in a chair by the fire. He was one of the few amongst us who rejoiced in the possession of a tolerably decent pair of boots. In order to keep them from flying to pieces, he had sent for me to put a few stitches in them, but I was so utterly wearied that I refused to have anything to do with them. But the officer took off his boots and insisted I get out my wax threads and mend them. He got up from his chair and he and his servant thrust me into it. They put the boots into my hands, got out my shoemaking implements, and held me as I attempted to cobble up the boots. It was in vain. I tried my best and managed a few stitches but fell asleep as I worked, the awl and wax-ends falling to the ground. Two other officers were present - Lieutenants [John] Molloy and Keppel[9], the latter of whom soon afterwards fell dead from fatigue. They all saw how pointless it was to urge me to mend Lieutenant Hill's boots and he therefore put them on again. With a woeful face and a curse, he dismissed me to my repose.

Our rest was of short duration. The French were upon our trail, and before long we were up and hurrying onwards again.

As the day began to dawn, we passed through another village - a long, straggling place. At that early hour, the houses were all closed and the inhabitants mostly buried in sleep, probably unconscious to the armed thousands who were pouring through their silent streets. A couple of miles from this village, Craufurd halted us for about a quarter of an hour. He must have wanted to have a good look at us in the returning daylight for he mingled amongst us as we stood leaning upon our rifles. He gazed earnestly in our faces as he passed, trying to judge our plight by our countenances. He himself appeared anxious, but full of fire and spirit as he occasionally gave directions to the different officers, and spoke words of encouragement to the men.

I am proud that, in passing, General Craufurd seldom omitted a word to myself. On this occasion he stopped in the midst and glanced down at my feet:

"What, Harris! No shoes, I see?"

"None sir," I replied. "They have been gone many days."

He smiled and passed on, speaking to another man, and so on through the whole body.

Craufurd was terribly severe if he caught the men pilfering. During this short halt, a very tempting turnip-field was close to us. Several of the men were so ravenous that, although he was in our very ranks, they stepped into the field and helped themselves to the turnips, devouring them like famished wolves. This time, Craufurd either did not, or would not, observe the delinquency and soon afterwards gave the word for us to move on once again.

I remember another sight which I shall not forget to my dying day. Even now it causes me a sore heart to remember it. Soon after our halt beside the turnip-field, the screams of a child drew my attention to one of our women, who was endeavouring to drag along a little boy of about seven or eight years of age. The poor child was completely exhausted, his legs failing under him. Up to this moment, the mother had occasionally been assisted by some of the men, who had taken it in turns to help the little fellow on, but now all appeal was in vain. No man had more strength than that necessary for the support of his own carcass. Although the mother could no longer raise the child in her arms - as her reeling pace too plainly showed - still she continued to drag the child along with her. It was a pitiable sight, and it was wonderful to behold the efforts the poor woman made to keep the boy amongst us, even though she was like a moving corpse herself. At last, the little fellow had no strength even to cry. With mouth wide open, he stumbled onwards until they both sank down to rise no more. When the shades of evening came down, they were far behind, amongst the dead and dying.

I witnessed similar scenes amongst the women and children during that retreat. Poor creatures! How bitterly the women must have regretted accompanying their husbands into Spain instead of accepting the offer to embark at Lisbon for England, but they are most persevering in such cases, and are not to be persuaded that their presence is often a source of anxiety to the corps they belong to.

I remember another incident which may have been a couple of days after the punishment of Howard. We came to a river which was tolerably wide, but not very deep. This was just as well for had it been deep as the dark regions, we would have had to go through somehow or other, for what with the avenger behind, and Craufurd along with us, we were kept moving along whatever the obstacle. So into the stream went the light brigade, and Craufurd, busy as a shepherd with his flock, rode in and out of the water to keep his wearied band from being drowned as they crossed over. One officer, probably to save himself from being wet through, and having to wear damp breeches for the remainder of the day, had mounted the back of one of his men. Craufurd spied him. The sight of such effeminacy was enough to raise the choler of the general and he was soon plunging and splashing through the water after them.

"Put him down, sir! Put him down! I desire you to put that officer down instantly!" Whereupon the soldier dropped his burden into the stream like a hot potato and went on through.

"Return, sir," said Craufurd to the officer, "and go through the water like the others. I will not allow my officers to ride upon the men's backs through the rivers. All must take their share alike here."

Wearied as we were, this affair caused all who saw it to almost shout with laughter. It was never forgotten by those who survived the retreat[10].

General Craufurd was one of the few men apparently created for command. During such dreadful scenes as we were familiar with in this retreat, he seemed to be made of iron. Nothing daunted him, nothing turned him from his purpose. War was his very element, and toil and danger seemed to call forth an increasing determination to surmount them.

It sometimes amused me to see him with the Rifles always at his heels, like they were his familiars. When he stopped his horse and halted to deliver one of his stern reprimands, you would see half a dozen lean, unshaven, shoeless, and savage Riflemen leaning on their weapons, scowling up in his face as he scolded them. And then, when he dashed the spurs into his reeking horse, they would throw their rifles upon their shoulders and hobble after him again. He was to be seen in the front, and then in the rear, and then you would fall in with him again in the midst. Sometimes he would be dismounted, and marching on foot, so that the men could see he took an equal share in the toils which they were enduring.

Craufurd took a mortal dislike to a commissary. Many a time I heard him storming at the neglect of those gentry because the men were starving for rations, yet nothing but excuses was forthcoming.

"Send the commissary to me!" he would roar. "Damn him! I will hang him if provisions are not up this night!"

Craufurd was twice in command of the light brigade. The second time he joined them after they had been some time in Spain. I heard that it was then that he said something like this:

"When I commanded you before, I knew full well that you disliked me, for you thought me severe. This time I am glad to find there is a change in yourselves."[11]

CHAPTER 11

Retreat to Vigo
2 January - February 1809

The events Harris next describes happened, he says, on the evening of the day Daniel Howard was flogged which, according to Surtees, probably occurred on 2nd January.

Towards the evening of the day Howard was punished, we came to a part of the country which was even wilder and more desolate than that which we had already traversed. At that inclement season it was a dreary wilderness and in spite of the vigilance of the General, many of our men resolved to stray into the open country rather than traverse the road before them. The coming night favoured their designs, and before morning many were lost to us through their own wilfulness.

I too found myself completely bewildered and lost upon the heath, and should doubtless have perished had I not fallen in with another of our corps, who was in the same situation. He was James Brooks, a strapping fellow from the north of Ireland. He was delighted at having met with me, and we resolved not to desert each other during the night.

Brooks became my companion in adversity. He was a strong, active, and resolute fellow - as in Portugal I had on more than one occasion witnessed - and his strength was useful to both of us.

"Catch hold of my jacket, Harris," he said, "for the ground here is soft. We must help each other tonight, or we shall be lost in the bogs."

And before long, that is what happened. Brooks found himself stuck so fast in the morass that although I used my best efforts to draw him out, I succeeded only in sharing the same disaster. In our wearied state, this was an unlucky chance, and I turned and endeavoured to save my own life if possible, calling to him to follow before he sank in over head and ears.

It was dark, and we did not know which way to gain a firmer foundation. The more we floundered, the faster we fixed ourselves. Poor Brooks was so disheartened that he actually blubbered like a child. Then, during a pause in our exertions, just as we were about to abandon ourselves to our fate, coming down on the wind I thought I heard the bark of a dog. I bade Brooks listen. We both heard it distinctly and the sound gave us new hope. I had found some hard tufts of grass in the direction I tried, and I advised Brooks to lay himself as flat as he could, and drag himself out of the slough. By degrees, we gained a firmer footing. We eventually succeeded in extricating ourselves, but were in such an exhausted state that for some time we lay upon the ground helpless, and unable to proceed.

At length, and with great caution, we ventured to move forwards in the direction the sounds had come from, although our situation was still very perilous. In the darkness, we hardly dared to move a step in any direction without first probing the ground with our rifles, lest we should again sink and be smothered by the morasses into which we had strayed. As we carefully felt our way, we heard voices in the distance, shouting out 'Men lost! Men lost!': the cries of others in a similar situation

After a while, far away, I thought I saw something like a dancing light, similar to a Jack-o' lantern. It seemed to flicker about, vanish, and reappear. I pointed it out to Brooks and we agreed to alter our course and move towards it. As we did so, the light seemed to approach us, and grow larger. Another appeared, and then another. At first they looked like small twinkling stars, then more like the lamps upon

one of the London bridges seen from afar. The sight
revived our spirits, and we could now distinctly hear
the shouts of people, who appeared to be in search of
stragglers. As they approached us, we perceived that
such was indeed the case, and that the lights were
furnished by bundles of straw and dried twigs, dipped
in tar and tied on the ends of long poles. They were
borne in the hands of Spanish peasants from a village
near at hand. On reaching and halting in this village,
Craufurd, discovering that numbers of men had
strayed from the main body, had immediately ordered
the torches to be prepared. Collecting together a party
of Spanish peasants, he had obliged them to go out into
the open country and seek his men. By this means he
saved many from death that night.

Surtees says that, at ten that night, the main body
of the brigade reached the village of St. Domingo-
Flores, which he describes as a small village where
nothing could be procured except a very small quantity
of black bread: *'Tired with the journey, we felt rather
inclined to sleep than eat; and wet and dirty as we were,
we laid ourselves down till dawn.'*

When Brooks and myself reached the village, we
found it filled with soldiers standing and lying, huddled
together like cattle in a fair. They presented an
extraordinary sight as the torches of the peasants
flashed upon their wayworn and gaunt figures.

Soon after I reached our corps, I fell helplessly to
the ground. I was in a miserable plight, and it was
raining. Brooks too was greatly exhausted, but he
behaved most nobly by remaining beside me, trying to
persuade some of our men to lift me up and help me to
shelter in one of the houses at hand.

"May I be damned," I heard Brooks say, "if I leave
Harris in the streets to be butchered by the cowardly
Spaniards the moment our division leaves the town."

At length he succeeded in getting a man to help
him and together they got me into the passage of a

house, where I lay upon the floor for some time. With the help of some wine they procured, I rallied and sat up. Eventually I got once more upon my legs and, arm in arm, we went again into the streets and joined our corps.

Poor Brooks certainly saved my life that night. He is one of the many good fellows I have seen out. He was afterwards killed at Toulouse by a musket-ball which struck him in the thigh[1]. As I sit at my work in Richmond Street, Soho, I often think of him with feelings of gratitude.

The next day's march was towards Rua.

When the division got the order to move again, we were still linked arm in arm, and thus we proceeded. Sometimes we would stop for a short time to rest ourselves before hurrying on again. I remember Lt. Hill passing me on a mule. He wore his cloak and had a Spanish straw hat on. He seemed sorry for me for he knew me well. When he had passed, he looked back and said:

"I see you cannot keep up, Harris. Do your best, my man, or you will fall into the hands of the enemy."

As that day wore on, I grew weaker and weaker, and in spite of all my efforts, the main body left me hopelessly in the lurch. Brooks was getting weaker too. Seeing it was of little use to urge me on, he assented at last to my repeated request to be left behind, and without a word of farewell, he hurried on as well as he was able.

I soon sank down in the road. I lay beside a man who had also fallen, and who appeared to be dead. He was one of our sergeants, a man named Taylor, who belonged to the Honourable Captain (now General Sir Hercules) Pakenham's company. Whilst we lay there exhausted, the rear guard approached. They were endeavouring to drive on the stragglers, and a sergeant of the Rifles came up and stopped to look at us. He ordered me to rise; but I told him it was useless to trouble himself about me as I was unable to move a step further. The officer in command of the rear guard also came up. It was Lieutenant Cox, a brave and good man[2]. Observing that the sergeant was rough toward me in his manner and his language, Lt. Cox silenced him.

"Let him die quietly, Hicks. I know him well and he's not the man to lie here if he could get on. I am sorry, Harris, to see you reduced to this, for I fear there is no help to be had now."

He then moved on and left me to my fate. But after lying still for awhile, I felt somewhat restored and sat up to look about me. The sight was by no means cheering. On the road behind me I saw men, women, mules, and horses, lying at intervals, both dead and dying. Far away in front I could just discern the enfeebled army crawling out of sight, the women huddled together in the rear, trying their best to get forward amongst those of the sick soldiery who were unable to keep up with the main body. Some of these poor wretches cut ludicrous figures for although their clothing was extremely ragged and scanty, and their legs were naked; they had the men's greatcoats buttoned over their heads. They looked like a tribe of travelling beggars.

After a while, I found that the sergeant who lay beside me had also recovered a little, and I tried to cheer him up. I said that opposite where we were lying was a lane down which we might find some place of shelter, if we could muster enough strength to explore it. The sergeant consented to make the effort, but after two or three attempts to rise, gave it up. I was more fortunate and with the aid of my rifle I got to my feet. I saw death in my companion's face, and as I could render him no assistance, I resolved to try and save myself.

I hobbled some distance down the lane and, to my great joy, espied a small hut or cabin, with a little garden in its front. I opened the small door of the hovel, and was about to enter when it occurred to me that if I did so I might be knocked on the head by the inmates. As the rain was coming down in torrents, and to stay outside was to die, I resolved to try my luck within. I had little strength left, but determined to sell myself as dearly as I could, I brought up my rifle and stepped across the threshold.

Immediately, I observed an old woman seated beside a hearth, where a small fire burned. She turned her head. Seeing a strange soldier, she arose and filled the hovel with her screams. I drew back within the doorway. An elderly man, followed by two other men who were apparently his sons, rushed from a room in the interior and approached me. I brought up my rifle again, cocked it, and bid them keep their distance. Thus I brought them to a parley and getting together what little Spanish I was master of, I begged for shelter for the night, and for a morsel of food. I lifted my feet and showed them a mass of bleeding sores. They held a tolerably long conversation among themselves before consenting to give me shelter, but only on the condition that I left before daylight. I accepted with joy. Had they refused me, I would not be here to tell the tale.

All they gave me was some coarse black bread, and a pitcher of sour wine, but to a half-famished man it was acceptable, and I felt greatly revived by it. While I devoured the food, they sat and stared at me. Knowing the treachery of the Spanish character, I had refused to relinquish possession of my rifle, and my right hand was ready in an instant to unsheathe my bayonet.

Whilst I supped, the old hag, who sat close beside the hearth, stirred up the embers to afford them a better view of their guest. They overwhelmed me with questions, which I either could not comprehend or had not the strength to answer. I made signs that I was unable to maintain the conversation, and begged them as well as I could to show me some place where I might lay till dawn.

The place they permitted me to crawl into was like an oven, being nothing more than a sort of berth scooped out of the wall. It was so filled with fleas and other vermin that I was stung and tormented most miserably all night long. Such was the fear I entertained of having my throat cut by the savage-looking wretches still seated before the fire that, despite the weariness which pervaded my whole body, I was for some time unable to sleep except in fitful snatches.

Bad as my lodging and supper had been, they did restore me somewhat, and with the dawn I crawled out of my lair, left the hut, and retraced my steps along the lane to the high-road, where I found my companion, the sergeant, lying where I had left him the night before. He was dead.

A solitary individual, seemingly left behind amongst those who had perished, I now made my way along the road in the direction our army had retreated the night before. It was still raining, and as I passed them on the line of the march, even the dead looked comfortless in their last sleep. Had Heaven not given me an iron constitution, I think I would have failed on this day, for the solitary journey, and the miserable spectacles I beheld, rather damped my spirits.

After progressing some miles, I came up with a cluster of poor devils - men and women - still alive but unable to proceed. They were sitting huddled together in the road, their heads drooping forward, as though waiting patiently for their end.

Soon after passing these unfortunates, I caught up with a party which was being urged forward by an officer of the 42nd Highlanders. He was pushing them along pretty much as a drover would keep together a tired flock of sheep. It was a curious-looking party being composed of men of various regiments. Many had thrown away their weapons and were without shoes. Some were bare-headed; others had their heads tied up in old rags and fragments of handkerchiefs. To support one another, they were linked together arm in arm like a party of drunkards.

I marched in company with this party for some time, but because of my night's lodging and refreshment I was in better condition and ventured to

push forward in the hope of rejoining the main body.
This I succeeded in doing in the streets of a village.

The village may have been Rua, which the brigade
reached on night of 3 January, and where they rested.
Surtees confirms that during the two days' march from
Ponferrada, want and fatigue had compelled many men
to fall out. He assumes that most perished in the snow
or were captured, but relates how others rejoined them
at Rua after having obtained 'some little refreshment
from the local people', as Harris had done.

Falling in with the Rifles, I again found Brooks. He
was surprised to see me alive. We entered a house, and
begged for something to drink. At this time, I had on
my back a shirt I had purchased of a drummer of the
9th regiment before the commencement of the retreat.
It was the only good one I had. With the assistance of
Brooks, I stripped, took it off, and exchanged it with a
Spanish woman for a loaf of bread which Brooks,
myself, and two other men shared.

During this part of the retreat I noted Craufurd,
who was not a whit altered in his desire to keep the
force together. He was as active and vigilant as ever,
but now seemed to keep his eye upon those who were
most likely to hold out. This day, I marched close
beside him for many hours. He looked stern and pale,
but the very picture of a warrior. I shall never forget
Craufurd if I live to be a hundred years. He was in
everything a soldier.

Craufurd's interest in the freshest men was
practical because Lt. Cox states that, on 4 January, a
detachment of three hundred of the them were sent
ahead by forced marches to Orense to secure the bridge
over the River Minho.

The autobiographers and diarists who were on the
retreat to Vigo, have little say about events between 4
January and 7/8 January (when the light brigade

arrived in Orense), except to refer to days of incessant marching *"through almost impassable roads, without baggage, which no doubt took the road of the main column, and benighted far short of our destination, which was sure to be wretched villages half buried in snow, and [therefore] frequently having to feel with poles for doors of the houses. Fortunate were they who found any provisions in them, for too often the inmates, when they found the men coming, absconded after concealing all eatables. They also drove away their oxen, which caused great difficulty in getting bullocks for the sick carts."* (Cox)

Surtees said that at Orense: *"we remained a day and obtained provision, then much needed by us all, for the men had been literally starving for several days past. We had time also to strip and change our linen, (that is, those who had a change); the others washed the shirts they took off, sitting without one till it was dry."*

The rest at Orense refreshed the men and on the 9th they crossed the Minho and continued to Ribadavia, arriving about midnight. From Ribadavia their route was through Puenteáreas.

Slowly and dejectedly our army crawled along, their spirit of endurance considerably worn out. I felt that if the sea was much further from us, we would come to a halt without gaining it, for I felt something like the approach of death. A sort of horror was mixed up with my sense of illness, a reeling I had never experienced before, nor since. I held on, but despite all my efforts, the main body again left me behind. Had the enemy's cavalry come up, I think they would have had little else to do but ride us down. It is astonishing how man clings to life, for had I lain down I am sure that spot would have been my last billet.

Suddenly I heard a shout in front and it became prolonged in a sort of hubbub. Even the stragglers dotting the road in front of me seemed to catch something like hope. As the poor fellows reached the top of the hill we were ascending, there was the occasional exclamation of joy, the first note of that sort we had heard for many days. When I reached the top of the hill the scene spoke for itself - far away in our front, the English shipping lay in sight.

It was not until 12 January that the exhausted soldiers had their first view of the sea at Vigo, and of the English shipping awaiting them there. Surtees: *'I do not remember ever [witnessing] a sight which inspired me with greater pleasure than the shipping and the sea did on this occasion... The fleet of transports for the army under Sir John Moore was just clearing the bay as we came in sight, but we observed that a sufficient number remained at Vigo to transport us to our native land, a place we sorely longed for.'*

This view acted as a restorative to our force. At the prospect of a termination to the march, the men plucked up spirit for a last effort. Fellows like myself, who hardly had strength in their legs to creep up the ascent, seemed now to pick up a fresh pair to get down it with. Such is hope to us poor mortals!

In the Rifles there was a man called Bell. During the day he had been holding a sort of creeping race with me, and we had passed each other as our strength served. He was rather a discontented fellow at the best of times so, during this retreat, he had given full scope to his ill-temper, cursing the hour he was born, and wishing his mother had strangled him at birth in order to have saved him from his present toil. For some time he had not spoken, but the sight of the English shipping had a very beneficial effect upon him. As he stood and looked at it, he burst into tears.

"Harris," he said, "if it pleases God to let me reach those ships, I swear never to utter a bad or discontented word again."

We went down the hill and met, for the first time during the retreat, symptoms of good feeling from the inhabitants. A number of old women stood on either side of the road handing us fragments of bread as we passed.

It was now, whilst I looked anxiously upon the English shipping in the distance, that I found my eyesight failing. It alarmed me to think that I was fast growing blind, and I made desperate efforts to get on, but Bell won the race this time. He was a very athletic and strong-built fellow, and left me far behind[3].

I believe I was the very last of the retreating force to reach the beach, though doubtless many stragglers were left behind, having come up after the ships had sailed. I managed to gain the sea-shore, but it was only by the aid of my rifle that I could stand. My eyes were now so dim and heavy that it was with difficulty I made out a boat, which seemed to be the last to put off.

Fearful of being left in the lurch half-blind, but unable to call out, I took off my cap and placed it on the muzzle of my rifle as a signal. Luckily Lieutenant [William?] Cox, who was aboard the boat, saw me and ordered the men to return. Making one more effort, I walked into the water. A sailor, stretching his body over the gunwale, seized me as if I had been an infant, and hauled me on board. His words were characteristic of the English sailor:

"Hello there, you lazy lubber! Who the hell do you think you are that we should hang around all day for you?"

The boat was crowded with our exhausted men. They lay helplessly at the bottom, and every moment the heavy sea drenched them to the skin. As soon as we reach the side of the vessel, the sailors helped us to get on board, which in our exhausted state was no easy matter. They were obliged to place ropes in our hands, set their shoulders under us, and heave us up as if we were bales of goods they were pushing on board.

"Heave away!" cried one of the boat's crew, as I clung to a rope. "Heave away you lubber!"

But I was quite unable to pull myself up. The tar placed his shoulder beneath me as he spoke, and pushed me up against the ship's side. I lost my grasp of the rope, and had two of the crew not grasped me, I would have fallen into the sea. They drew me into the port-hole like a bundle of foul clothes. My belt and bayonet, torn off in the effort, fell into the sea. I lay where the sailors placed me and within minutes was sound asleep.

The first troops to reach Vigo were embarked on 12 January. They included Surtees: *"It was my fortune to be sent on board the* Alfred, *a 74, with two of our companies."* The remaining companies of the 2nd battalion were put aboard the *Aid* transport, and the *George and Mary*. Lt. Cox was aboard the latter. Was Harris aboard her too? The English shipping remained at anchor in Vigo from 12 to 20 January, awaiting orders. The delay enabled many stragglers to rejoin them.

Surtees: *A great number of men were still behind, for the last few days' marches had deprived us of many who, till then, had braved the toils and privations of the journey, but who now had fairly sunk under exhaustion. The Commodore, therefore, remained as long in the bay as it was safe, sending the stragglers as they arrived on board the different ships; but within a few days of our arrival, the enemy entered the town, which of course precluded all hope of more escaping."*

They sailed from Vigo on 21 January.

I slept long and heavily, and was awoken only by the terrible noise and bustle on board, for a gale had sprung up. As night came on, the wind increased and we were soon experiencing all the horrors of a storm at sea - the sails were torn to shreds, the coppers overset, and the pumps were kept at work incessantly, night and day, till they were choked. All the time the gale grew worse and worse. I thought we were going to go to the bottom.

The soldiery were ordered below, and the hatches closed. Soon after, the vessel turned over on one side and lay a helpless log upon the water. To give the vessel a chance of righting herself in the roaring tide, we had to be kept on the side which was uppermost, so an officer was placed over us. He had a sword in one hand, and a lantern in the other. His task was not an easy one because the heaving waves frequently sent us sprawling from the part we clung to, over to the lowermost part of the hold where he stood, so he was obliged to keep driving us back. We expected every instant to be our last. In this painful situation we remained for about five or six hours then, to our great joy, the sea suddenly grew calm, the wind abated, and the vessel righted herself. We were once more released from our prison, having tasted nothing in the way of food for at least forty-eight hours.

Soon after, we arrived in sight of Spithead. There we saw nine of our convoy which, laden with troops, had been driven on shore in the gale. We remained off Spithead for five or six days. One fine morning, we received orders to disembark, and our poor bare feet once more touched English ground[4].

The inhabitants who flocked down to the beach to watch must have been a good deal surprised at the spectacle we presented. Our beards were long and ragged, and almost all of us were without shoes and stockings. Many had their clothes and accoutrements in fragments, and some had their heads swathed in old rags. Our weapons were covered with rust. Quite a few men, from toil and fatigue, had become quite blind.

Among the Riflemen who came ashore with Harris were John, Michael and Peter Hart:

In the Rifles, there were three brothers named Hart - John, Mike, and Peter - and three more reckless fellows never existed. Nothing escaped their notice, and even when advancing under the hottest fire of the enemy, with their comrades being shot down beside them, they would create the greatest fun and laughter. At Vimeiro, Lieutenant [John] Molloy - himself as fine a 'soldier as ever stepped, and as full of life in the midst of death' - was obliged to check them.

"Damn you!" he told them. "Keep back, and get under cover! Are you running into the teeth of the French thinking you are going to fight with your fists?"

Those three men could run like deer, and during the time we remained in Portugal I never saw them the worse for hard work, having been formed by Nature and disposition for the hardships, difficulties, and privations of the life we then led. All three, however, were pretty well done up during the retreat to Corunna, but even in that dreadful business, their light-heartedness, and attempts at fun, kept up the spirits of many a man who would otherwise have been broken-hearted. As we disembarked upon the beach at Portsmouth, they made a jest of their own appearance, and of the miserable plight of the whole turn-out:

"We look more like the rakings of hell than the fragments of an army!" one of them observed.

Nothing, I suppose, could exceed the dreadful appearance we cut when we disembarked from Corunna. The inhabitants of Portsmouth, who had assembled in some numbers to see us land, were horror-stricken that their countrymen, and their relatives, were returning to England in such a ghastly state.

But don't think we were to be despised as soldiers. Long marches, inclement weather, and want of food had done their work upon us, but we were perhaps better than we appeared. Under the gallant Craufurd we had made some tremendous marches, and even galled our enemies severely making good our retreat by the way of Vigo. And our comrades in adversity, those under General Moore who had retired by the other road to Corunna, had turned to bay there, and showed the enemy that the English soldier is not to be beaten even under the most adverse circumstances[5].

The three Harts had their feet swathed in bloody rags, and their clothing hardly covered their nakedness. Their accoutrements were in shreds.

Beards covered their faces, and their eyes were dimmed with toil. Their arms were nearly useless, the rifles being encrusted with rust, and the swords glued to the scabbard. Yet these three brothers hobbled up the beach, cracking jokes upon the misery of our situation, and the appearance they themselves cut. I heard them myself.

Nothing but Flushing, that unwholesome fen, that grave of battalions, could have broken the spirits of three such soldiers as John, Mike, and Peter Hart. A few weeks in that country sufficed to quiet them for evermore. One died. The other two were never worth a rush afterwards, but remained as living examples of what climate can do to a strong constitution and a body apparently framed of iron[6].

I also recollect at this time [after arriving at Portsmouth] an affecting display of female affection. As he disembarked from the boat, one of our officers - whose name I will not mention, but who was much beloved by us all - observed his wife waiting for him on the beach. She rushed into the sea to embrace him. He met her and they were locked in each others' arms before they touched the dry land.

Rifleman Richard Pullen and his family also took part in the retreat. Pullen had joined the 95th on 7th September 1806, in the same recruiting exercise in Ireland which had netted Harris.

Whilst we [ie the new recruits and the recruiting party of the 95th] lay near Cork, we were joined (amongst others) by Richard Pullen who, having exchanged from the English militia into the Irish, volunteered to us Rifles from the North Mayo. He brought with him little to boast of but his wife and two children: Charles, a mischievous boy of about twelve, and Susan, a pretty little lass about fourteen years of age. They all went with us to Copenhagen, and got through the expedition pretty well.

Major Robert Travers

William Cox

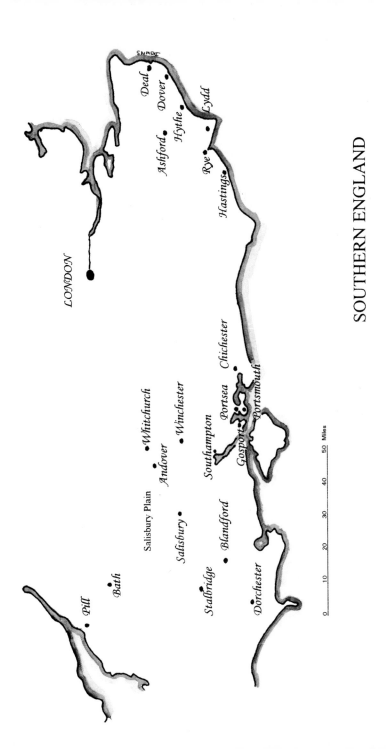

SOUTHERN ENGLAND

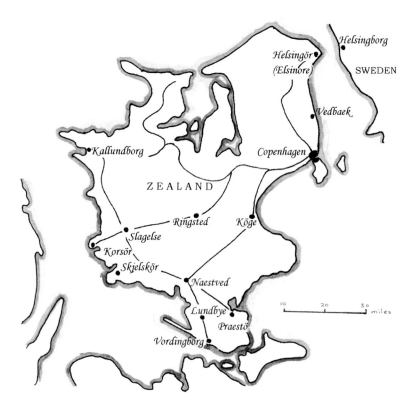

DANISH EXPEDITION
August - October 1807

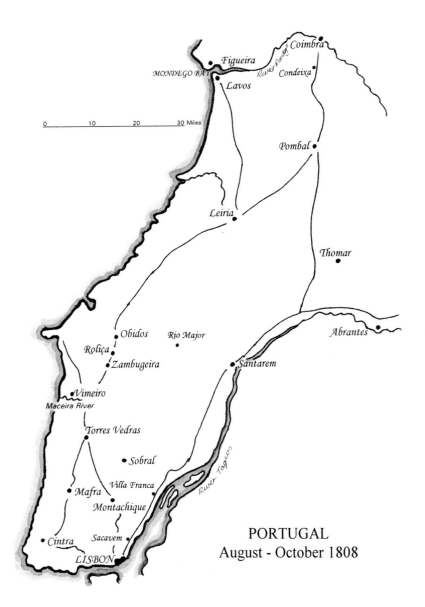

Coimbra

Figueira

River Mondego

MONDEGO BAY

Condeixa

Lavos

0   10   20   30 Miles

Pombal

Leiria

Thomar

Obidos   Rio Major

Abrantes

Roliça

Zambugeira   Santarem

Vimeiro

Maceira River

Torres Vedras

Sobral

River Tagus

Villa Franca

Mafra

Montachique

Cintra   Sacavem

LISBON

PORTUGAL
August - October 1808

Corunna

Lugo

SPAIN

Ponferrada •

• Astorga

R. Minho

• Orense

Sahagun

La Beneza •

• Villada

Vigo

Mayorga •

• Villalon

Benevente •

• Villa Major

Zamora

Toro

• Valladolid

PORTUGAL

• Tordesillas

Porto

R. Douro

• Salamanca

Almeida •

R. Mondego

• Coimbra

• Pombal

TO LISBON

CORUNNA CAMPAIGN
October 1808 - January 1809

Madrid •

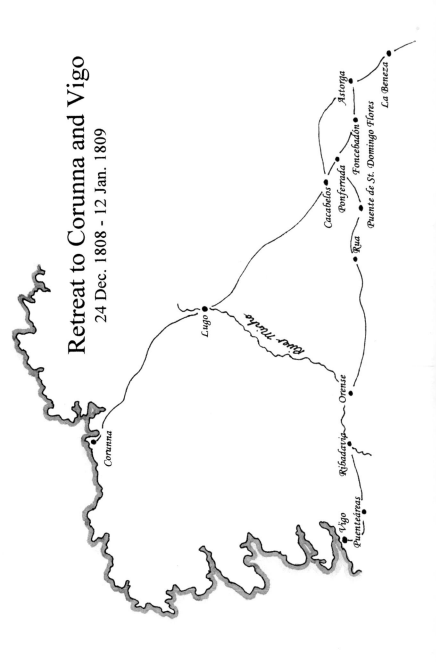

Retreat to Corunna and Vigo
24 Dec. 1808 - 12 Jan. 1809

Corunna

Lugo

River Miño

Vigo
Puenteáreas

Ribadavia

Orense

Rua

Cacabelos
Ponferrada
Foncebadón
Astorga
Puente de St. Domingo Flores
La Beneza

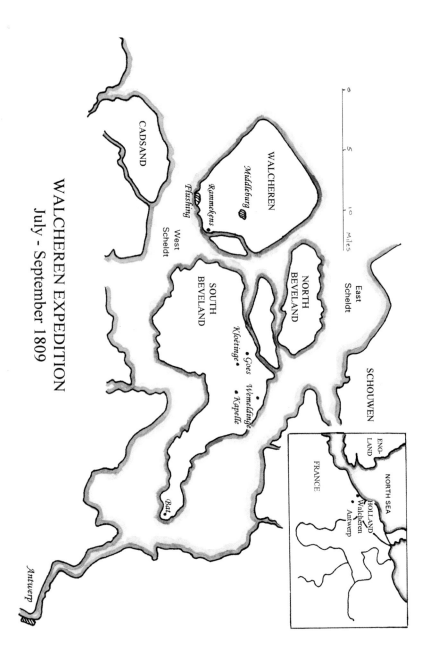

WALCHEREN EXPEDITION
July - September 1809

CADSAND

WALCHEREN

Middleburg

Flushing *Rammekens*

West Scheldt

East Scheldt

NORTH BEVELAND

SOUTH BEVELAND

Kloetinge *Goes*

Wemeldinge

Kapelle

Bat.

SCHOUWEN

Antwerp

0   5   10
Miles

ENG- LAND

NORTH SEA

FRANCE

HOLLAND
Walcheren
Antwerp

That affair suited a man of Pullen's description, for he didn't like too much service, and we soon found he was rather a shy cock. When he was lagging behind on the march, constantly flung in his teeth was: 'None of your North May*ho* here, Master Pullen!'

In 1808, when our four companies went to Portugal, Pullen was again wanted but begged off on account of the wife and two children. From then until we were well away from Hythe, he therefore had to endure again the taunt of 'None of your North May*ho* here, Master Pullen!' At Sahagun, amongst the Rifles that came fresh from England, we found Pullen, his wife, and Charles and Susan. The meeting caused no small fun amongst us, and for a few days North May*ho* was again the bye-word.

On the first day of the retreat to Corunna, Pullen looked very chapfallen and seedy, and was beginning even then to complain that he could not stand much more. His wife and children were also dropping behind. The poor souls thought that when night came on they would be billeted, but the open world was now their only refuge. At that time, there was no allowance to stop or lie down, even on the bare heath.

When I saw Pullen again on the third or fourth day, neither the wife nor children were with him, nor could he tell where they were. He could answer only for himself, and said that at every step he expected to drop dead. That's all I saw of Pullen, his wife and children, or even thought of them (for I had enough to do the keep my own strength up), but when we landed at Portsmouth, to my surprise, we saw Pullen once more. Much we wondered at the sight of him when so many better and stronger soldiers had died before half the retreat was accomplished, but we did not have enough spirit left to jeer him about North May*ho*.

To add to poor Pullen's dejection, he knew nothing of the fate of the wife and children he had left behind, and as the men continued to disembark, there was Pullen inquiring anxiously of every one for some tidings of them. None could he get. At last, however, he saw his wife coming up the beach, and hobbled off to meet her. They inquired of one another for Charles and Susan. As he had trusted they were with the wife, and she had hoped they were with the husband, they both sat down upon the beach and cried in concert.

Our men thought it useless, but they continued their enquiries, never failing to ask after their offspring of every person they fell in who had been in that retreat. About a fortnight later, they advertised in the public newspapers. We all laughed at the idea and told them they might have spared the money, so it was no small surprise to us, therefore, that the artillery at Plymouth answered their advertisement. They stated that while upon the mountains of Spain, they had heard a little girl screaming at night and had taken care of her as well as they could. They had her with them. The description answering, she was forwarded to Hythe, and Pullen and his wife once more embraced their daughter Susan. Of the boy no tidings came.

Soon after the retreat, Pullen's wife gave birth to a child, having confessed long before her belief that it was French on its father's side. She related to many of us her adventures on the retreat and, among other things, told how she and other women, having taken refuge in a barn, had been overtaken in the night by the French and treated in a very unceremonious manner[7].

It is easy to suppose that Mrs Pullen had no great wish to go on active service again, and much did she endeavour to persuade Pullen to evade it too, but with the whole regiment under orders for Walcheren, he was unable to. He did however try to excuse himself by tampering with his eyes. He made them sore by putting snuff in them, but was detected and disgraced. He sailed with the expedition and died in that dreadful country of Walcheren, with many a gallant soldier for his fellow victim[8].

After his death, Mrs Pullen and her daughter were sent to their parish in Warwickshire. She had been gone some time when a letter arrived. It was from her son Charles, who was a prisoner in France. The bugle-major opened it, and on enquiry found that I alone knew the parents of the writer. Crampton, Pullen's captain, was dead, and the company was almost entirely new. I think I was the only man left in the regiment who recollected the North Mayho recruit, war, pestilence, and discharge having taken the rest away. At the time I myself was almost in a dying state and the matter was soon forgotten altogether. No answer that I ever heard of was sent to poor Charles, so whether Mrs Pullen ever again saw her son, I cannot take upon me to say.

CHAPTER 12

Recruiting and Recruits
Spring 1809

The Riflemen who survived the Corunna campaign returned to Hythe. The total loss to the 2nd battalion is difficult to arrive at but at least two sergeants and seven Riflemen had died from wounds or exhaustion. Forty-four men, including Sitdown and Higgins, were missing. According to Verner, some of those taken prisoner by the French subsequently escaped and made their way to Portugal.

> After the disastrous retreat to Corunna, the Rifles were reduced to a sickly skeleton. Out of about nine hundred fellows, as active and fine as any who fought in an enemy country, we paraded some three hundred weak and crestfallen invalids. I stood the third man in my company, which was reduced from nearly a hundred men to *three!* On that first parade, hardly any of the companies were stronger than ten or twelve men. Over the next few parades, we were augmented as our sick companions gradually recovered, but some of those who did not sink in hospital were never again of much service as soldiers.
>
> As the captain of my company [Leach] was sick, it was Lieutenant Hill who commanded the three men who answered for No.4. He smiled when he looked at me.
>
> "Harris," he said, "you look the best man here this morning. You seem to have got over this business well."
>
> "Yes sir, thank God. I feel pretty stout again now, which is more than many can say."

Both battalions of the Rifles had been in that retreat. The first battalion, commanded by Colonel [Thomas Sidney] Beckwith, then lay at Colchester. Ours (the second), commanded by Colonel Wade, was quartered at Hythe. The 43rd and 52nd regiments paraded with our battalion at Hythe on this occasion. Both had been with us on the Corunna retreat and therefore cut as poor a figure as we did.

In Spring 1809, orders were received by the 95th to recruit for both battalions. Surtees was sent to Ipswich, where the Northumberland Militia (to which he had once belonged) was based, and Harris was selected for a party which was to recruit locally, in Kent and Sussex.

After a while some of the strongest and smartest of our men were picked to go recruiting to gather men from the militia regiments, so that
our ranks might be filled up. I was one and I started off with Lieutenant Pratt[1], Sergeant-major [Thomas] Adams, and William Brotherwood.

As a shoemaker in the corps, I had saved up twenty pounds, which I had in my pocket. With the money I hired a gig, in which the sergeant-major and myself cut very smart figures. Unfortunately, neither of us could drive very well and we therefore overturned the gig on the first day when our journey was only half-way completed. The shafts being broken we left the gig behind us in a small village midway between Hythe and Rye, and were obliged to take to our legs, as was more soldierly and seemly. We reached Rye the same night and there I got the first recruit.

I entered the tap-room of the *Red Lion* where sat a fellow whose appearance I was struck with, for he was a chimney sweep who had with him a little boy as black and sooty as himself. His name was John Lee. He was strong and able-bodied and offered to enlist immediately. I took him at his word, and immediately called for the sergeant-major for his approval.

"There's nothing against my being a soldier but my black face," said the sweep. "I'm strong, active, and healthy, and can lick the best man in this room."

"Hang your black face," said the sergeant-major; "the Rifles can't be too dark. You're a strong rascal, so, if you mean it, we'll take you to the doctor to-morrow and make a giniril [general] of you the next day."

That night we got the sweep into a large tub of water, scoured him outside, filled him with punch inside, and made a Rifleman of him. The sergeant-major, however, suspected from his countenance that Lee was rather a slippery fellow (which afterwards turned out to be the case), and that he might repent so, after getting him drunk, he said to me:

"Harris, you caught this bird, so you must keep him fast. Tonight you must sleep handcuffed together in the same bed, or he will escape us."

This I did, and next morning I retraced my steps, taking him to Hythe to be passed by the regimental doctor[2].

After rejoining sergeant-major Adams at Rye, we set off for Hastings in Sussex. On our way we heard that the East Kent Militia was at Lydd, so we stopped there about an hour, displaying ourselves before them, and trying to coax a few of them into the Rifles.

In those days, the men on recruiting service were accustomed to make as gallant a show as they could, so we had both smartened ourselves up a trifle. The sergeant-major was quite a beau; he had a sling belt to his sword like a field-officer, a tremendous green feather in his cap, a flaring sash, and his whistle and powder-flask were displayed. There was an officer's pelisse over one shoulder, and he had a double allowance of ribbons in his cap. I was as smart as I dared appear, with my rifle slung at my shoulder. In this guise we made as much of ourselves as if we had both been generals, and arm in arm we strutted up and down before their ranks, creating such a sensation that the militia-men cheered us until they were called to order by the officers. The permission to volunteer had not then been given to the East Kent, although it came out a few days afterwards, but during that hour, we persuaded many that the Rifles were the only boys fit for *them* to join.

That same night, we reached Hastings where we found that the volunteering of the Leicester Militia (who were quartered there) had commenced. One hundred and twenty five men and two officers had given their names to the 7th Fusiliers, and Adams and I determined to try to make these men change their minds in our favour. The appearance of our Rifle uniform, and a little of Sergeant Adams' blarney, so took the fancy of the volunteers that we got every one of them, and both officers, for the Rifle corps.

We worked hard in this business, and for three days and nights kept up the dance and the drunken riot[3]. Every volunteer got ten guineas bounty. Two were kept back for necessaries, but the rest they spent in every sort of excess till all was gone. Then came the reaction - the drooping spirits, and the grief at parting with old comrades, sweethearts, and wives, for the uncertain fate of war. Then there were the jeers of the old soldiers, the laughter of Adams and myself, and their comrades, and we attempted to give a fillip to their spirits as we marched them off from the friends they were never to look upon again. '*Shoving them on to glory*' is what we termed it, and it was a glory they were not long in achieving, for out of the hundred and fifty of the Leicestershire we enlisted in Hastings, there was scarcely a man left at the year's end who could not show some token of the fields he had fought in. Very many found a grave; others returned to Hythe with the loss of their limbs.

The 95th recruiting parties were so successful that a third battalion was formed, and it was into this that the names of those who were still missing after the Corunna retreat, were placed.

I remember the stories of many of these men, and one in particular. His name was Deaman and I enlisted him myself. A smart and very active man, he was serving as a corporal in the light company of the Leicestershire Militia when I persuaded him to join our corps. He was immediately made a sergeant in the third battalion, then just forming. The cause of Deaman's merits being first noticed was not a little curious because it was a race, got up at Shorncliffe[4] soon after he joined, amongst some Kentish men noted for their swiftness. One man, who had beaten his companions, challenged any soldier in the Rifles to run against him for £200. The sum was so large, and the runner of such celebrity, that although we had some active young fellows, none - neither officers nor men - seemed inclined to take the chance. But then Deaman stepped forth. He said he would run against this Kentish boaster, or indeed any man on the face of the earth, and fight him afterwards into the bargain, if someone would make up the money. Upon this, an officer subscribed the money, and the race was arranged.

The affair was quite a sensation, and inhabitants in villages from miles around flocked to see the sport. The men from different regiments of infantry, cavalry, and artillery, who were in the neighbourhood, were also much interested and managed to be present, so the scene was a very gay one.

The race commenced. At the start the odds were much against the soldier, who did not look at all like a winner, but who kept up well with his antagonist. The race seemed likely to end in a dead heat when, close to the winning-post, Deaman gave a tremendous spring forward to win by his body's length.

The race led to Deaman's notice, and his promotion. General [Kenneth] Mackenzie, who was in command of the garrison at Hythe and who was present, was delighted at the Rifleman beating the bumpkin. He saw that Deaman was a very smart fellow and well cut out to be a soldier.

News of the race then reached the first battalion fighting in Spain where Sir Andrew Barnard was then in command of the Rifles. I heard that when either he, or some other officer of rank, was told of the race, he remarked that as Deaman was such a smart runner in England there was very good ground in Spain for him to use his legs, and he was accordingly ordered out with the next draft. In Spain, Deaman so distinguished himself that he obtained his commission in one of our line regiments, although which one I cannot now remember[5].

I could give many more anecdotes connected with recruiting for the three battalions of Rifles at this time, but the above will suffice.

Soon after this incident, with our companies now full of young and active men, we started off with the expedition for Walcheren, which had just been formed. When we paraded, and I stood enranked for this expedition, I could not help feeling that I was amongst strangers, for of all the men in the company to which I belonged, only James Brooks had been a fellow comrade in the fields of Portugal and Spain.

The huge number of recruits obtained, and the subsequent formation of the 3rd battalion, led to a complete reorganisation of the regiment, after which the 1st battalion was sent back to the Iberian Peninsular. It embarked at Dover on 25 May 1809. With it went two transfers from the 2nd battalion - Captain Jonathan Leach and Lieutenant William Cox.

I felt too the loss of my old captain, whom I loved and respected, and who had just left the second battalion to be promoted in the first. When I heard of this, I stepped from the ranks and offered to exchange too, but Lieutenant Hill, who was present, hinted to Captain [John] Hart, my new commanding officer, that if he let me go he might repent of it. My character had been so good in the former campaign that Captain Hart was persuaded to keep me, and I accordingly remained in the second battalion, and started on the Walcheren expedition.

CHAPTER 13

The Walcheren Expedition
July - September 1809

At the battle of Trafalgar in October 1805, Nelson had
defeated the French so decisively that their naval power
was crippled, and it became necessary for them to build
new ships in order to rebuild their navy. One of the
places chosen for this work was their base in the
Scheldt, a large winding river flowing through the
Dutch province of Zealand (now in Holland), which had
many dockyards, and gave easy access to the English
Channel. The danger of the siting of this French base
was not lost on the British Government, and the merits
of seizing the Scheldt estuary, the island of Walcheren,
and the port of Flushing, had been considered since at
least 1797. In April 1807, the project was revived by
Robert Stewart, Viscount Castlereagh, the new
Secretary of State for War and the Colonies, who feared
that French naval power in the area would become so
great that it would prove a threat to southern England.
He drafted proposals for a expedition, but military
demands elsewhere caused them to be shelved.

By early 1809, as Castlereagh had feared, the
Scheldt had become the second largest French naval
arsenal in Europe. It was possible for ninety warships
to be housed in its harbours and ports. Alarmed,
Castlereagh revived the idea of an expedition and urged
an immediate attack. His plan was adopted but the
expedition was delayed because many of the troops
needed for it were either ill, or ill-equipped, as a
consequence of the Corunna retreat. However, by July

1809 everything was ready. The fleet which had been assembled consisted of 264 warships and 352 transports of different sizes. The 44,000 troops which were to sail with it were under the command of John Pitt, the earl of Chatham. So extensive was the military undertaking that it was referred to in the English press as the Grand Expedition. Part of the 95th, including Harris' company, was chosen to accompany it.

From Hythe to Deal was one day's march, and I remember looking along the road at the good appearance of the different regiments as we marched along. I had never seen such a fine expedition - the army seemed to stretch all the way before us to Dover.

The ill consequences of having so many women amongst us in our former campaign and retreat had been so apparent that for the Walcheren expedition the allowance of wives was considerably curtailed therefore, at Deal, when the Rifles embarked in a seventy-four called the *Superb*, there was a terrible outcry from them upon the beach. The distraction of the poor creatures at parting with their husbands was quite heart-rending. Some clung to the men so resolutely that the officers were obliged to give orders to have them separated by force. The screaming and howling of their farewells rang in our ears after we were in the boats, and even far out at sea.

The weather was fair, and the fleet having a grand and imposing appearance, many spectators (some from as far as London) came to look at us as we lay in the Downs. We set sail in three divisions about three days after our embarkation[1]. A fair wind carried us off Flushing, where one part of the expedition disembarked. The other part - myself among them - made for South Beveland.

In 1809, the Dutch province of Zealand consisted of the islands of Walcheren, North and South Beveland, Schouwen, and other smaller islands, which supported 121 towns and villages. It was on the largest island,

Walcheren, that the port of Flushing was located. Most of the islands were protected from the sea by a network of dykes, but there were frequent floods, and the terrain was so low that some drainage ditches never emptied. Stagnant water was much in evidence, even in summer.

The first objective for the British soldiers on the expedition was the occupation of Walcheren and South Beveland, and for this purpose the invading army was separated. Harris was with Sir John Hope's division, part of which was landed near Wemeldinge on South Beveland on 1 August 1809. Within two days, all of South Beveland was in British hands. On Walcheren, Flushing, though besieged, held out for two weeks.

Five companies of the 95th were landed on South Beveland on 9th August. With them was Major-General William Stewart who wrote in his diary that the weather was so hot that, as they marched to their quarters in Wemeldinge, some men fell sick and were left by the side of the road:

"The 95th did not enter this quarter until nearly six o'clock, the heat and late inactivity on shipboard having enervated them, and caused many to lie speechless on the sides of the road."

About South Beveland, Stewart wrote: *"Nothing can exceed the goodness of the roads or the richness of the country through which our whole march was conducted. The country is one low level, and excepting that it is well wooded, resembles the richest part of the Isle of Ely. [There is] not a spot which is not cultivated and laid out in rich corn, beans or pasture... and for comfort and cleanliness nothing can exceed the houses of the poorer orders. The partiality, or rather bonhomie, which the inhabitants showed to our troops was very striking."*

The five companies of Rifles immediately occupied a very pretty village, with rows of trees on either side of its principal streets. There we had plenty of leisure to listen to the cannonading going on amongst the companies we had left at Flushing.

The appearance of the country, such as it was, was extremely pleasant, and for a few days the men enjoyed themselves. But in less than a week, an awful visitation came suddenly upon us[2].

The first I knew of it was when I was sitting in my billet and beheld, in the street, whole parties of our Rifleman shaking with a sort of ague to such a degree that they could hardly walk. The shaking, which seized their whole bodies from head to heel, was so great that strong young men who had been but a short time in the service, seemed suddenly reduced in strength, and unable to stand upright.

The company I belonged to was quartered in a barn, and I quickly perceived that hardly a man there had stomach for the bread served out to him, or a taste for his grog (each man having an allowance of half a pint of gin per day). About three weeks after we landed, I and two others were the only individuals who could stand. The rest lay groaning in rows in the barn, amongst the heaps of lumpy black bread they were unable to eat.

This awful spectacle considerably alarmed the officers, many of whom were also attacked. The naval doctors came on shore to assist the regimental surgeons, who had more upon their hands than they could manage. Dr Ridgeway of the Rifles, and his assistant, had nearly five hundred patients prostrate at the same moment. In short, except for myself and three or four others, the whole concern was completely floored[3].

The doctors were confounded and, since all hope of getting the men on their legs seemed gone, orders were issued to embark them as fast as possible. This was done with some difficulty, although the poor fellows made every effort to get on board. Those who were a trifle better than others crawled to the boats. Some supported each other, but many were carried helpless as infants.

At Flushing matters were not much better, except that there the soldiers had a smart skirmish with their enemies before the fever and ague attacked them.

The fever, which had started on South Beveland, quickly spread to Walcheren. So many soldiers fell sick from it that the army's strength was seriously reduced. Flushing held out long enough to allow time for the French to reinforce Antwerp, which Lord Chatham no longer had enough fit men to attack. He was left with no option but to terminate operations.

By 30 August, when the evacuation of troops from South Beveland began, 3,000 men were sick, many of whom were embarked with the healthy. Still the fever continued to spread, and with such rapidity that, two days later, 6,000 men were incapacitated.

On 1 September, four companies of the 2nd battalion were embarked on the *Ulysses*, off Wemeldinge. The remainder were embarked on smaller vessels and transferred to the *Sceptre*. By 8 September, when the fleet finally sailed for England, 11,000 men of the Grand Expedition had succumbed to the illness.

On shipboard matters did not improve; the men began to die so fast that ten or twelve were committed to the deep in one day. It was extraordinary that myself, Brooks, and a man named Bowley[4], who all three had been at Corunna, should at that moment have been free of the disease and that, despite the awful appearance of the pest-ship we were in, I had little fear of it. I thought it could not touch me because I was so hardened.

Men being scarce, I stood sentinel over the hatchway, and Brooks - who even in the jaws of death was a jolly and jeering companion - came past me. It was pudding-day aboard ship, and he offered me a lump. It was at that moment that I was struck with a deadly faintness. I shook all over like an aspen. My

143

teeth were chattering in my head, and I could hardly hold my rifle.

Brooks looked at me for a moment, the pudding in his hand. He saw I could not take it.

"Why Harris, old boy, *you* are not going to begin, are you?" he said.

As I trembled, I could only mutter: "For God's sake get me relieved, Brooks!"

"So it's all up with Harris," he said. "You are caught hold of at last, old chap!"

I was soon sprawled upon the forecastle amongst many others. We were in a miserable state, with our knapsacks and our great-coats over us. During our short voyage, the doctors were fully employed, and pails of infusion of bark were carried amongst us and given to the men in horn tumblers. Thus we arrived at Dover. As I lay on the deck, I looked up at the splendid castle in the distance. It was identified with old England and many a languid eye was cheered by its sight. Men naturally love to die upon their native land, and I felt I could now do so contentedly. I have in my eyes now that frowning English fortress as I then beheld it.

The Warwickshire Militia, who were quartered at Dover and came to assist in our disembarkation, were obliged to lift many of us out of the boats like sacks of flour. If any of those militiamen remain alive, they will not easily forget that duty, for I never beheld men more moved than they were at our helpless state. Many men died at Dover and more in Deal. Those who rallied on getting from the land of pestilence were paraded in order to get them to their old quarters at Hythe[5].

All in the 43rd and 52nd regiments who were able marched with us this day to Hythe; but I'm afraid none of us cut much of a figure on the road. In fact, such was the shaking fever we felt, we were pretty much left to get to our journey's end in the best manner we could. Several times I sat down exhausted by the roadside. When I looked at the men and saw how awfully disease had enfeebled them, I thought how similar it looked to the Corunna retreat. Many would never have got into barracks without assistance.

So filled with sick was the hospital at Hythe, that the barracks also became a hospital. As deaths ensued and thinned the wards, the men were continually removed, progressing from barrack to hospital, and from hospital to the grave[6].

I was in a ward of the hospital which accommodated eleven men. As they died, I was gradually removed until I was driven up into a bed in a corner of the ward. Here I lay and saw this ward refilled ten times, the former patients being all carried out to the grave. I had plenty of leisure to observe my comrades in misfortune, and witness their end. Some I beheld die quietly; others were seized in various ways. Many got out of bed in the night in a shivering delirium and died upon the floor. One or two of my old Peninsula comrades, men I had often seen fighting bravely on the field, I saw die in this hospital in a miserable condition, their bodies swollen up like barrels.

Having been a shoemaker in the Rifles, I had, during my service, saved up nearly £200. It was in the bank at Hythe and it enabled me to procure extra wine and other nourishing things for myself, and to give my companions in misfortune a treat. I think it was this which enabled my iron constitution to keep death at bay so long.

Everything was done for us that skill could devise. Nothing could exceed the kindness and attention of Dr Ridgeway towards us. Hot baths were brought into the hospital - many a man died whilst in the bath.

As I lay sick, I heard that our comrades were dying so fast that firing over their graves was being dispensed with. When I got out, I went to the churchyard to look upon their graves. There they lay in two lines. As in life they had been enranked, so they lay also in similar order in death.

The medical men made every effort to trace the immediate cause of this mortality amongst us. Almost all the men were examined after death, but to no avail, for nothing could arrest the progress of the malady after it had reached a certain height. I heard that, in most cases, the doctor generally attributed the deaths to enlargement of the spleen, as almost all were swollen and diseased in that part. I myself was dreadfully enlarged in the side, and for many years afterwards carried an 'extra paunch'[7].

The disease from which the men originally suffered was malaria, which is caused by a parasite transmitted by the bite of a mosquito. Malarial parasites travel in the blood stream to the liver where they multiply rapidly within cells which then burst, releasing more malarial parasites into the blood stream. The symptoms are severe fever, cold sweats, shivers and/or rigors. Left untreated malaria can cause death. In those who survive, it can recur intermittently causing fevers, general ill health and anaemia.

In Harris' time, the doctors were unsure of what was causing the illness and therefore had no effective remedies. However, according to medical studies conducted soon after the return of the expedition, the situation was exacerbated by overcrowded conditions in barracks, hospitals and on transport ships, which led to outbreaks of dysentery, typhus and typhoid. John Webbe, the inspector of hospitals, who himself became a victim, submitted a perceptive report which suggested that the fever would probably be recurring and have long-range effects, which was without doubt the case, as both Harris and John Kincaid testify.

The hazards of the Walcheren area in July and August were known to the English authorities because soldiers previously stationed there had suffered from fevers, but never before had the disease developed into the epidemic proportions experienced by those who took part in the Grand Expedition. 4,000 men died from illness alone, and 12,000 were incapacitated. There was an outcry in England about the failure of the expedition, and a crisis in Government ensued. Recriminations were so great, and passions so strong, that a duel was fought between the Foreign Secretary and the Minister of State for War.

CHAPTER 14

Invalid
1810-1813

The Walcheren Expedition, though a disaster, did not bring an end to British involvement in the wars in Europe. Instead, the British Government decided to concentrate the military effort against the French on the Iberian Peninsula. The objective was to liberate Portugal and then Spain, and extra money was made available for the additional troops which were required.

Sir Arthur Wellesley had returned to Portugal in April 1809 as commander of the English troops still stationed in and around Lisbon, and in May 1809 the 1st battalion of the 95th was despatched to join him. It was to be many months before the 2nd battalion could muster enough fit troops to send after them, such were the debilitating effects of Walcheren fever.

As soon as the prospect began to brighten, and the men to recover a little, some three hundred of us managed to muster outside the hospital, parading there morning and evening to benefit from fresh air. Medicine was served out to us as we stood enranked, the hospital orderlies passing along the files giving each man his dose from the large jugs they carried.

As we got better, an order arrived to furnish two companies of the second battalion and two companies of the third battalion of Rifles, for Spain, where they were much wanted. Accordingly an inspection took place and two hundred men were picked out. All were most anxious to go. I myself was rejected as unfit, which I much regretted. However, after a few days, on making application, I was accepted, principally on the recommendation of Lieutenant [Thomas] Cochrane, who much wished for me. In consequence, I once more started for foreign service.

From Hythe to Portsmouth, where we were to embark, was eight days' march, but the very first day found out some of the Walcheren lads. That night I myself was assisted to my billet, the ague having again seized me. On the third day waggons were requisitioned to get us along the road. As we proceeded, some of the men who had relapsed died by the way, and were buried in the different places we passed through. A man died beside me, and at Chichester he was taken out of the waggon and buried.

I was told that, in Spain, the Great Duke [of Wellington], observed that several men who had come out from England after Walcheren were unable to keep up on the march, and afterwards completely failed. He inquired the reason of this, and was told they were men who had been on the Walcheren expedition.

"Then never," said the Duke, "let another man be sent here who has been at Walcheren."[1]

At Portsmouth, I remained one night, billeted with my fellow-travellers at the *Dolphin*. There I was visited by an uncle who resided in the town. He was much shocked at seeing me. Such was the sad state we were again reduced to, he concluded that I was unlikely to survive many days[2]. The next morning, spring-waggons were procured for us and we were sent back to Hilsea barracks for medical advice. I took a farewell of my uncle expecting never to see him again. Such, however, was not to be the case - out of the thirty-nine Riflemen who went into Hilsea hospital, I alone survived.

If it seems extraordinary that I should twice be the survivor of so many of my comrades, I can only refer the reader to the medical men who attended us, if they are still alive - Dr Ridgeway of the Rifles, and Dr Fraser, who was the surgeon at Hilsea.

Whilst we lay sick at Hilsea hospital, an act of great kindness and humanity was performed towards the soldiery by Lady Grey who was, I believe, the wife of the Commissioner of Portsmouth Dockyard. She was so struck with the state of the sufferers that, one morning, she sent two carts loaded with warm clothing for them. To each man who had been at Walcheren, no matter of what regiment, she gave two pairs of flannel drawers and two flannel waistcoats. This was greatly appreciated by the men and many, like myself, have never forgotten it.

After this, and being the only Rifleman left at Hilsea, Lieutenant Beddell[3] made application to the general for leave for me to go into Dorsetshire to see my friends. Although this was granted, the doctor shook his head, doubtful that I would be able to endure the journey. About a week later, I considered I was fit enough to undertake it.

I was put into a Salisbury coach by a non-commissioned officer of one of the line regiments. We started about four o'clock, and my fellow passengers inside were a lady and gentleman. They did not relish being in close quarters with such a sick-looking soldier. Indeed, we had hardly cleared the town of Gosport when I gave them a dreadful fright by being attacked all at once by one of my periodical ague-fits. I shook to so desperate a degree that they were horror-struck, and were inclined to keep me company in my trembling! The lady, expressing herself as most unhappy at having begun her journey that day, thought they would certainly catch the complaint, and that she and her husband were lost. The coachman, guard, and the passengers outside, by no means liked it either.

These fits generally lasted an hour and a quarter, when a burning fever would come on. During this I called for water at every place the coach stopped.

"Here's a nice go," said the coachman when he stopped at a place called Whitchurch. "You won't catch me taking up a sick soldier again if I can help it. This here poor devil's going to die in my coach."

It seemed as if I had personally offended the burly coachman, for he made an oration at every place he stopped, and sent all the helpers and idlers to look at me, until I begged him not to do so.

I had two attacks during the night, and was so bad that, like the coachman, I thought I would not get out of the vehicle alive. Never had passengers so unpleasant a journey as the lady and gentleman I travelled with.

Early in the morning, the coach stopped at a village one mile from my father's residence on the estate of the present Marquis of Anglesey[4]. Although I was a boy when I left my father's cottage[5], I knew the landlord of the little inn where the coach stopped, and several other persons I saw there, but none recognised me. I was terribly exhausted so I made myself known as well as I could, and the landlord immediately got four men to carry me home[6].

My father was much moved at beholding me returning in so miserable a plight, as were my stepmother and my brother[7]. I remained with them eight months, and for six of them lay in bed in a hopeless state. During that time, Captain Hart sent four letters to the commanding officer, desiring me to be drafted out to Spain where, being a handicraft, I was much wanted, but every month certificates were sent to Hythe stating my inability to move. Hearing of my state, many of the neighbourhood medical men came to see me to observe the nature of a complaint that had proved so fatal to our soldiers.

At the end of the eight months, I was somewhat recovered and able to crawl a few yards from our cottage door with the aid of stick. As my stepmother had once or twice expressed herself burthened by this long illness, I resolved to attempt to return to my regiment and I was therefore transported in a cart to the *King's Arms Inn* at Dorchester where the surgeons of the 9th and 11th Dragoons examined me. My body was swollen up hard as a barrel, and my limbs were covered with ulcers, so they ordered me into

Dorchester hospital, where I remained seven weeks[8]. My case completely puzzled the faculty. At length Dr. Burroughs, on making his rounds, caught sight of me sitting on my bed, dressed in my green uniform.

"Hallo Rifleman," he said, "how came you here?"

Being told, he looked very sharply at me, and seemed to consider. "Walcheren, eh?"

"Yes sir," I said, "and it has not done with me yet."

"Strip, my man," he said, "and lie on your back. What have you done for him?" he asked sharply of the doctor.

The doctor told him.

"Then try him with mercury, both externally and internally," said Dr. Burroughs in a rapid manner, and turning quickly, he proceeded on his rounds amongst the rest of the patients.

I was now salivated most desperately, after which I got a little better. But I was so utterly tired of the hospital life I had so long led that I resolved, at all hazards, to try and rejoin my regiment.

"For Heaven's sake!" I said, "Let me go and die with my own regiment."

With some difficulty I got leave to go, and once again started by coach, at my own expense, for Hythe in Kent. Before doing so, however, and to my surprise, the medical man who had attended me under my father's roof brought me in his bill. It was a pretty good sum for a poor soldier to be charged - £60! Having enough left of my savings, I paid it, but I kept the bill, and afterwards showed it to Dr. Scott of the Rifles.

"It could not have been higher, Harris, if you had been a man possessing a thousand a year," he remarked[9].

When I made my appearance in the barrack-square at Hythe, I was like one risen from the dead. I had been missing so long from amongst the few I knew there, that I was almost forgotten. It was a hardy Scot named McPherson, who recognised me first[10].

"Eh, my certie," he said, "here's Harris come back. Why, I thought, man, ye was gane amangst the lave o' them, but the de'il will na kill ye, I think!"

The day after my arrival I was once more in hospital, and here I remained for twenty-eight weeks under Dr. Scott. Such was the Walcheren fever that, to this day, in damp weather, I sometimes feel the remains of it.

CHAPTER 15

Soldiers of the 95th

Throughout the original recollections, Harris dotted his narrative with anecdotes about fellow riflemen, most of whom were known personally to him. However, he was not an eye-witness to all of the incidents he described. In the sections about Roliça, Vimeiro and Corunna, there is no doubt that, for the most part, he narrated what he himself saw and knew, but his account of the activities of riflemen at Hythe and abroad from the end of 1809 to the culmination of his service with the 95th in early 1814, is largely second hand.

It should be remembered that, after Walcheren, he never went on active service again, and from December 1809 to December 1811 he was not even at the regimental base in Hythe, but sick in either Hilsea, Stalbridge or Dorchester. It is my belief that when he eventually returned to Hythe at the beginning of 1812, he caught up on news about the regiment, and that the majority of the stories now gathered together in this chapter, were told to him at that time by fellow riflemen like John, Michael and Peter Hart, whom the muster lists record as being at Hythe for some of the time during 1812 and 1813. They, or others like them, would have been quick to bring an old comrade like Harris up to date on the gossip from home and abroad.

Despite being second-hand, most of the tales appear to be accurate in essence if not always in detail. They are occasionally contradicted by riflemen whose first-hand testimony is more reliable, or by official records. All, however, are included here regardless.

Officers of high rank in the army of the Peninsula have been heard to say that there never were such a set of devil-may-care fellows, and so completely up to their business, as the 95th. It would be invidious to make a distinction or talk of any one regiment being better, or more serviceable, than another, but the Rifles were generally in the mess before the others began, and were the last to leave off. It was their business to be so. If they did their work well, so did every other British corps engaged in that country. At least I never heard, or saw, to the contrary.

Amongst us there was, perhaps, as intelligent and talented a set of men as ever carried a weapon. At times, they seemed to need but a glance at what was going on to know about its why and wherefore. The intelligence of these men was indeed very great, and I could relate instances of their recklessness and management which would amuse the reader much. I remember a fellow named [Thomas] Jackman getting close up to the walls at Flushing. He worked a hole in the earth with his sword and laid himself in it. There he remained alone, in spite of all the efforts of the enemy and their various missiles to dislodge him. Thus earthed, he was known to have killed with the utmost coolness and deliberation, eleven French artillerymen as they worked at their guns. As fast as they relieved each fallen comrade, so did Jackman pick them off, after which he took to his heels, and got safe back to his comrades.

During the Walcheren expedition Harris was on South Beveland not at the siege of Flushing, therefore this account of Dublin-born Thomas Jackman is second hand.

Thomas Mayberry [Meabrey] was a man well known at that time in the Rifles. He was a sergeant in my day, and much thought of by our officers as being a very active and useful non-commissioned officer. He was considered by them to be one of the most honest men in the army, although he was not so well liked by the men, who thought him boastful and tyrannical.

One day, whilst in the town of Hythe, he got hold of about £200, and in a very short space of time, managed to lose it in the society of a party of gamblers who at that time infested the town. A little time after, Captain Hart - who then commanded the company Mayberry belonged to - was not a little thunderstruck to find that several of the tradesmen who furnished articles for the men had not been paid. Sending for Mayberry, he discovered the delinquency. So well thought of had he been, that Captain Hart was as astonished as if his own father had committed a fraud. Mayberry was imprisoned and brought to court-martial with two soldiers he had seduced into becoming partners in his gambling transactions.

On further inquiry it was discovered that, for the last ten months, he had been in the habit of cheating the men of his company out of a farthing each a week. This was, perhaps, the worst thing against him and he was sentenced to receive seven hundred lashes. As Corporal [David] Morrisson and Patrick Divine were participants in this roguery, the former was awarded three hundred lashes, and the latter one hundred. When the square was formed for punishment, and the three were brought out, it was necessary to check the men of the regiment, who would have hooted and hissed them on the parade.

One of the civilians Mayberry had defrauded - a man called Gilbert - inquired the time of the punishment, having expressed to some of Mayberry's companions that he was content to lose the money if he could see the fellow well flogged, and he was therefore present in the rear during its infliction. This is pretty good proof that, when their own interests are closely concerned, your civilian has no objection to being an eye-witness to the floggings about which there has lately been such an outcry. Nowadays it is not uncommon to see a man who has committed crimes which have earned him the curses of his companions in arm, drummed out of the corps and then, without the barrack-gates, being received by a host of folks and taken to their bosoms as an object of commiseration.

When Mayberry was tied up he was offered, as was then customary, the option of banishment[1]. Notwithstanding the considerable entreaty to accept made to him by his two comrades, who thought that they too would escape the lash, he refused and decided to take the seven hundred.

He bore the sentence without a murmur. Not so the two others. Morrisson screamed and struggled so much that he capsized the triangle. All came sprawling together, so that he was obliged to be held by a man at each side.

Divine came last. He was rather an effeminate-looking man, and the colonel rode round and told him he lamented being obliged to break so fair a skin, but he must do his duty. As Divine had borne a good character, and was not so much to blame as the other two, he let him down after five and twenty.

After this, Mayberry was held in contempt by his fellow-soldiers, and ill-thought of by the officers. When a detachment was being sent to Portugal, he volunteered for the expedition, but Captain Hart was unwilling to take him because he now had such a bad opinion of him. However, Mayberry was so desirous of going that at last Captain Hart consented, and at the siege of Badajoz he wiped off all his former ill-conduct. He was seen by Captain Hart to behave so bravely in the breach that he commended him on the spot.

"Well done, Mayberry!" said he. "You have this day done enough to obliterate your disgrace, and if we live, I will endeavour to restore you to your former rank. Go now to the rear; you have done enough for one day."

Although covered with wounds - he was known to have killed seven men with his rifle sword-bayonet - Mayberry refused to retire.

"No going to the rear for me," he said. "I'll restore myself to my comrades' opinion, or make a finish of myself altogether."

He accordingly continued in the front of all, till at last, in the clear light of the fire-balls, he was seen to be cut down by a tremendous sword-cut, which cleft his skull almost in twain. Morrisson, I heard, also died at that siege. Divine returned safe home and died of fatigue at Fermoy.

The casualty returns for the regiment record that Sergeant Mayberry and Corporals Morrisson and Divine (Devine, Devayne) were all reduced to the ranks in late February or early March 1811, therefore their court-martial probably took place about that time. If so, Harris cannot have witnessed their punishment because he was sick in Hilsea. Nor was he present at the siege of Badajoz, being in Hythe in April 1812 when it took place. However, he must have known all three men reasonably well because in 1809 they had all been in his company.

Before joining the army, Thomas Mayberry had been a weaver in Kilkenny. He was promoted to sergeant on 3 April 1806, and remained a sergeant until 9 March 1811. Morrisson - who had joined in 1808 - and Divine, prior to their disgrace, had been corporals since 25 October 1809. Mayberry was indeed killed at the storming of Badajoz on 6 April 1812, but Morrisson was not, being promoted again to corporal on 1 September 1812 (and busted backed again on 6 March 1814). He was discharged on 6 January 1815. Divine was also reinstated as a corporal. As that happened on 7 April 1812, the day after the siege of Badajoz, perhaps he, like Mayberry, distinguished himself in the fighting but without losing his life? His elevation did not last long, however. He was reduced to the ranks again a year later, a pattern repeated in July 1814 and October 1815.

In about 1807 or 1808 a man volunteered into the Rifles from the Nottingham Militia. After the rifle regiment had served him half of his bounty, he declined to serve them in return, and made off without joining. Four years afterwards he was discovered by the man who had been a sergeant in his company of the Nottingham Militia when he had volunteered from them into our corps. It was while the sergeant was himself recruiting that he fell in with his former comrade in some town in Yorkshire, the name of which I forget.

The man (whose name, also, I have forgotten now) had grown very fat and was as much altered in dress as in condition, being clad in the habiliments of a respectable and comfortable farmer of that delightful county. But the sergeant had a sharp eye which penetrated the disguise of the man's calling, and not even the portly look could throw him off the scent. He went warily to work, making inquiries, comparing notes, and allowing for time and circumstances; then, notwithstanding the respectability and reputed worth of our farmer, he arrested him as a deserter from the 95th.

From Yorkshire he was marched a prisoner to Hythe in Kent. I remember seeing him brought in, handcuffed and guarded by a corporal and three or four men. He was dressed as he had been apprehended, being clad in his farmer's dress. This made myself and those others who happened to be out, more especially regard him because, although it was no great sight at that time to see a deserter in that situation, it was not often we beheld one who appeared to be so well off and respectable-looking. The Yorkshire farmer made a great talk amongst us. We pitied him much, and while awaiting his trial, he dwindled perceptibly in bulk every day.

During his confinement he wrote to the colonel of the regiment offering him £60 to be let off, but I don't believe he got any reply. He was tried and sentenced to receive seven hundred lashes.

When he was brought into the hollow square to receive his punishment, the anxiety amongst us was twice as great as on any other occasion of that sort. He did not seem to be afraid of the lash because of the

pain of its infliction but, considering the situation he
had attained, the shame it caused. Even though fallen
away - his flesh seemed to hang about him from the
quickness with which he had been reduced in bulk by
long marches, and by anxiety of mind - he was still a
jolly and portly-looking man. He addressed a few words
to the colonel in a firm and manly tone, and begged
him to consider his situation and circumstances, being
the husband of a respectable woman, and father of
several children. But it was not possible for the colonel
to forgive him, and he was ordered to be quick and
prepare. So the farmer stripped, and was tied up.

In addressing him, the colonel referred to the offer
he had made when in confinement which, because it
supposed the colonel capable of selling his honour for
£60, had much aggravated his crime. So the farmer
received his seven hundred lashes that day, and never
uttered a word of complaint during the infliction, except
to sometimes turn his head and look after the can of
water, when he would say:

"Poor Tom! Poor Tom! I little thought ever to come to
this!"

I remember that, after four hundred, the colonel
asked him if he would sign his banishment in foreign
parts, but he refused to do so, and the punishment
went on. The doctor desired the drummer to lay the
lash on the other shoulder, and the farmer received the
whole sentence, as he well deserved.

In a week or more he was to be seen walking in the
barrack-square, but he avoided the society of the men.
Then, two or three days afterwards, he was missing
altogether. He had taken an opportunity to escape, and
never again did we see, or hear of, the Yorkshire
farmer.

It is clear that, in this instance, Harris personally
witnessed the return to barracks of the Yorkshire
farmer, and his punishment, so this may have taken
place in 1812 or 1813.

There was another agriculturist in the Rifles with me, the eldest son of a gentleman-farmer who also resided in Yorkshire. He was very handsome, and although only about twenty-four or twenty-five, he was one of the wildest chaps in the whole country, as his parents found out to their cost. In one of his sprees he happened to fall in with Sergeant [Daniel] Sugden of our corps, and was not content until he had enlisted. Sugden, as you may easily conceive, was not averse to indulging him, and very soon had him for a recruit.

Although there must have been a considerable difference in the style of his life amongst us compared to what he was used to, he appeared in no way displeased with the change. In fact, at times, he was rather too lively a bird, and having plenty of money occasionally got himself into trouble, although nothing particularly disagreeable. He was very much liked in the corps, in which he went by the name of 'The Gentleman Farmer', although I cannot now remember his name.

Just before a detachment of the Rifles started for Portugal, a gentleman rode into the barrack-square and inquired after this young spark of some of the men. The eventual meeting between the two was not very amicable for the newcomer was the brother of the Gentleman-Farmer, who was upbraided with his conduct in enlisting, and told of the anxiety and sorrow it had caused at home. After they had become mollified, they sought an interview with our commanding officer, and in the name of the parents, the brother offered to pay any reasonable sum the colonel chose to name to grant the Gentleman Farmer a discharge. But the colonel was not willing to lose him and refused to grant the request.

"He is a wild and untamed spirit," he said; "and as he is just now under orders for foreign service, he had better go. Let him have a year of that fun. It will do his complaint good and if he lives, we shall, I hope, see him return an improved man."

The brother was compelled to put up with this answer, and the next morning, though much cut up and disappointed at his lack of success, he returned home to his parents. The Gentleman-Farmer embarked for Portugal and was soon witness to a wilder scene of discord and horror than even his hair-brained ideas quite contemplated when he enlisted for a soldier. He took his first lesson in actual warfare at the siege of Badajoz where, entering with heart and soul in the breach, his head was dashed into a hundred pieces by a cannon ball.

It has not been possible to identity this man, who may have served in any one of the three battalions of the 95th, all of which suffered casualties at the siege of Badajoz.

In the Rifles was an officer named, I think, Cardo [Daniel Cadoux]. He was a great beau, and although rather effeminate and ladylike in manners - so much so as to be remarked by the whole regiment - he was a most gallant officer when we were engaged with the enemy in the field. Amongst other jewellery, he wore on his finger a ring worth 150 guineas. He was killed whilst fighting bravely in the Pyrenees. As he lay dead on the field, Orr, one of our Riflemen, observed the sparkling gem and immediately resolved to make a prize of it, but the ring was so firmly fixed, Orr could not draw it from the finger so, whipping out his knife, he cut the finger off by the joint.

After the battle, Orr offered the ring for sale amongst the officers. On enquiry, the manner in which he had obtained was learned. As a consequence, Orr was tried by court-martial and sentenced to receive five hundred lashes, which sentence was carried into execution.

According to Surtees, Captain Daniel Cadoux was killed in fighting near San Sebastian on 31 August

1813, soon after an engagement in which Spanish troops had forced the French to retreat:

"The enemy, being beaten, were obliged of course to retrograde. It came on one of the bitterest nights I have ever witnessed. The rain fell in torrents, and the lightning was very vivid. The French endeavoured to retrace their steps during the night, fording the river where they had crossed it in the morning; but the heavy rain had so swollen the river by midnight, that they could not continue any longer to wade it. A considerable number of them still remained on the other side, and no way presented itself of extricating themselves, but by forcing their passage across the bridge near which a company of our 2nd battalion, under Captain Cadoux, was posted, with one [company] of ours a short distance in the rear, to support him. Captain Cadoux's people were stationed in houses about thirty yards from the bridge, and had a double sentry on the bridge. The enemy's column approached very quietly, and then made a rush; but the rain having wet the priming of the sentries' rifles, they could not get them to go off to give the necessary alarm, and were in a moment driven from their post. The French then, seeing they had effected a passage, set up a shout, and rushed towards the houses where Cadoux's people were. They turned out at once, and with the supporting company, opened a deadly fire upon the enemy's column. But poor Cadoux fell instantly almost; as he had imprudently mounted his horse on the first alarm. His lieutenant also was severely wounded. The firing soon brought the whole brigade to the spot, which kept up a constant and well-directed fire during the whole of their progress along the little plains towards Vera."

Harris now relates details about a family of riflemen called Cumming or Cummings, previously transcribed as Comyn. The family probably consisted of Alexander, Joseph (bugle), Thomas (bugle), Allan, George, John, Hugh and William, although it is difficult to be certain because there were several other men with the same surname in the various battalions of the 95th at the same time. However, there can be no doubt that the Fluellyn Cummings referred to in previous editions is Allan Cummings, whose service record tallies well with Harris' account of it:

In the band of the first battalion of the Rifles we had a father and seven sons of the name of Cummings. The elder son, Fluellyn [Allan], was the best musician of them all, and on the regiment going on service to Portugal, he was made bandmaster. One night, whilst fighting against Massena, Allan Cummings took offence at a man named [Timothy] Cadogan, also belonging to our band, and catching him at advantage, beat him so severely that he left him for dead. The transaction having been seen by some of the soldiery, and supposing he had committed murder, Allan, fearful of the consequences, fled to Marshal Massena's army. There he was received kindly and, in consequence of his musical knowledge, was promoted to a good situation in the band of one of the French regiments. After a while, he made some mistake or other there, and the French army no longer being a safe place for him, he once more changed service. He returned amongst his old companions the Rifles where, to his surprise, he found Cadogan in the ranks, sound and well.

This species of inconstancy not being approved of by our leaders, he was tried by court-martial, and sentenced to be shot. I recollect that, at the same time, two or three other men, who had also committed heavy crimes, were under orders to undergo the same punishment. At that time, Colonel Beckwith was our lieutenant-colonel. Having a great respect for Allan Cummings' father, he made application to the Duke of Wellington for a pardon for his son. Accordingly, when he was brought forth amongst the other criminals, it was notified to him that, taking into consideration the interest made by his lieutenant-colonel, he should be forgiven. However I understand that the Duke desired it to be expressly stated to him that if he was ever detected in that country again in the garb of a soldier in the British service, nothing should save him from punishment. Cummings, therefore, left Spain, without the good wish of a single man in our corps, for he was pretty well known to be altogether a bad subject[2].

Meanwhile, the news having reached his friends in England that he had been shot, his wife quickly found a substitute, and when Allan thought proper - if somewhat tardily - to seek his home, he found her married again. At first the meeting was rather a stormy one, and the neighbours thought that murder would ensue, for Cummings found himself provided, not only with a *locum tenens*, but also with a little baby, neither of whom he could possibly have had any great liking for. Eventually, matters were amicably arranged and Allan, having made out his claim and satisfied the second husband that he had never had a musket-ball in his body, broke up the establishment and took his wife off to Hythe in Kent. There he again enlisted in the Rifles - in the third battalion - and joined them at Shorncliffe[3]. Once more he displayed his art, and from his excellence as a musician, was made master of the band. Not satisfied with his good fortune, he again misconducted himself, and was once more reduced to the ranks.

After a while he succeeded in getting exchanged to the 85th regiment. There too he managed to insinuate himself into the good graces of the commanding officer and, by his musical talents, once more also into the situation of master of the band. Here he might yet have retrieved himself, and lived happily, but he began to cut fresh capers. His ill-disposition and drunken conduct were so apparent the moment he got into an easy way of life, that it was not possible to keep him in the situation, and he was again reduced. He was eventually dismissed entirely as *too bad for anything*.

Meanwhile, one of his brothers had obtained the situation he held in the first battalion of the Rifles, and was greatly respected for his good conduct. He was killed at Vittoria, by a cannon-ball striking his head from his shoulders. As far as I know, the other five Cummings lived and prospered in the service. The old father was eventually discharged, and received a pension. What the ultimate fate of the bad sheep of this flock (Allan Cummings) was, whether he ever succeeded in becoming a band-master in the service of any other country, or whether he ultimately reached a still more elevated situation, I never heard, but it was not likely he ever came to good.

Allan Cummings was first promoted to sergeant from private on 25 October 1803 so he must have been an early recruit to the regiment. On 24 September 1809, he was reduced to the ranks for desertion. A year later, on 27 October 1810, he deserted again. This may have been the occasion he fled to André Massena, who was commander of a French army in Portugal in 1810 and 1811. He next surfaces in the regimental archives on 25 May 1813 when it is recorded that he was promoted from a private in the 3rd battalion to a sergeant, although by the end of the year he was a private again. On 21 February 1816, he was sent from the 3rd battalion at Hythe to the Isle of Wight for General Service.

Allan Cummings was not the only member of his family to decamp: Alexander deserted in 1802, and Joseph in August 1815. Thomas was transferred to the 3rd Veteran battalion in 1809, and a John Cummings died at Hythe on 25 September 1809, probably of Walcheren fever.

Some of Harris' information about the Cummings family postdates his departure from the regiment, which occurred in early 1814. This suggests he had contacts with former comrades as late as 1816 at least.

CHAPTER 16

Veteran

Harris was at Hythe from about December 1811 until
December 1813, when he was again sent into hospital.
Soon afterwards he was dispatched to Chelsea to be
assessed for a pension.

From Hythe, with some other invalids, I was sent to
Chelsea. Sixty of us marched together on this occasion,
and as many had had their limbs amputated due to
wounds and disease, our appearance was not
formidable. We were frequently obliged to halt in the
road to repair our strength, when the whole turn-out
would sit, or sprawl at full length, by the wayside.

This march took us ten days to accomplish, and
when we halted at Pimlico we were pretty well done up.
We were billeted in different public-houses in Chelsea,
and with others I lodged at the *Three Crowns*, close
beside the Bun House. We paraded in the Five Fields,
which was then an open space but is now covered with
elegant mansions and has become a part of London.
Three thousand invalids mustered here every morning.
It was a motley group, presenting a true picture of the
toils of war. There were the lame, the halt, and the
blind; the sick and the sorry, all in a lump. Those who
had lost their limbs did not have much trouble
becoming pensioners, but some of the others were
closely examined from day to day as to their eligibility
for service. Among others, I was examined by Dr.
Lephan.

"What age are you, Rifleman?" he said.

"Thirty-two, sir."

"What trade have you been of?" he enquired.

"A shoemaker," I replied.

"Where have you been?"

"In Denmark, Spain, Portugal, and Walcheren, in which place I met the worst enemy of all."

"Never mind that; you'll do yet. We will send you to a Veteran Battalion."

So, with others, I was appointed to the 8th Veteran Battalion and sent to Fort Cumberland. Here I joined the company of Captain Creswell, an officer who had lost one eye whilst in the 36th regiment in Spain. I was again the only green jacket of the lot, and as we had a great reputation in the army at that time, the officers assembled round me during the first muster and asked numerous questions about my service in the Rifles.

Major Caldwell, who commanded the battalion, had been in the 5th and had received a grievous wound in the head. He was a kind and soldier-like man, but if you put him out of temper you could see he felt his wound. Captain Picard was there too, and Captain Flaherty, and Lieutenant Moorhead. All of them were more or less shattered, and their men, although most were young, were good specimens of war's stern service. One had a tale to tell of Salamanca where he lost an eye; another spoke of the breach at Badajoz where he got six balls at once in his body. Many paraded with sticks in their hands, so they were a different sort of force to the active chaps I had been in the habit of serving amongst; and I was grieved at being obliged to part with my green jacket for the red coat of the Veterans.

At Fort Cumberland I remember a curious circumstance which might be thought worthy of narration. Many French prisoners had volunteered into the English service, and were formed into four companies called the Independent Companies. These men were smart-looking fellows, and wore a green uniform something like the Rifles. Whilst I was with the Veterans, one of these men deserted. He was retaken at Portsmouth, and tried by court-martial at Fort Cumberland. Besides his crime of desertion he had aggravated it by gross insubordination, and he was accordingly sentenced to be flogged. We were all - French and English - paraded to see the sentence carried into effect. The Veterans were all ordered to load with ball in case our neighbours, the green-jackets, showed fight. When the culprit heard the sentence read out to him he was a good deal annoyed, and begged to be shot as would have happened in his own country. It was explained to him that this could not be allowed, and he was accordingly punished. The Duke of York, who was then Commander-in-Chief[1], thought it necessary to make an example of him, although all of us would have been glad to see him forgiven.

The only court-martials of soldiers in the Independent Company of Foreigners recorded as occurring in the early part of 1814, took place at Lymington in February 1814 as a consequence of a violent and bloody affray in the High Street between a group of Frenchmen and some of the Royal Foreign Artillery. At least seven Frenchmen were court-martialled, but only one was found guilty. He was Jean Marie Soudinique. His sentence of 500 lashes on his bare back was laid before the Prince Regent for confirmation on 29 April 1814. As the punishment could therefore have been carried out during the period of Harris' service with the 8th Veteran Battalion - which was from 25 March to 10 July 1814 - was it Soudinique's flogging that he witnessed?

Shortly after this, Napoleon was sent to Elba, and these men were liberated and sent home to their own country. Four pounds were given to each man, and gloriously drunk they all were at Portsmouth the night they embarked. Having been quartered with the Frenchmen, the Veterans were very intimate and friendly with them, and we were therefore all sorry to hear - although whether true or not I cannot say - that on their return they were grossly maltreated by their fellow countrymen, their uniforms having betrayed their service to us.

I remained in the Veterans only four months because, at the expiration of that time, Napoleon was sent to Elba. We were marched to Chelsea to be disbanded, and there met thousands of soldiers lining the streets and lounging about before the different public-houses. They bore every description of wound and casualty incidental to modern warfare. Here hobbled the maimed light infantry-man and the heavy dragoon, there the hussar, the artillery-man, and the fusilier. There were specimens from every regiment of service. There was the Irishman, shouting and brandishing his crutch; and the English soldier, reeling with drink; and there was the Scot who, with grave and melancholy visage, sat on the steps of the public-house amongst the crowd, listening to the skirl of his comrades' pipes and thinking perhaps of the blue hills of his native land.

Such were Chelsea and Pimlico in 1814.

In about a week's time I was discharged, and received a pension of sixpence per day. For the first time since I had been a shepherd lad on Blandford Downs, I saw myself in plain clothes, and with liberty to go and come where I liked. However, before my pension became due, and in consequence of the escape of Bonaparte from Elba, I was, with others, again called upon to attend. But I was in so miserable a plight with the remains of the fever and ague - which still attacked me every other day - that I did not answer the call, and thereby lost my pension.

Harris was discharged on 10 July 1814, the army having no further use for his services. His discharge papers at the Public Record Office in Kew are filed with the records of the 8th Veteran Battalion, not with those of the 95th, with which he had seen the most service. As his discharge was due to him being unfit, and not on account of any vice or misconduct, he was recommended for the pension which he later forfeited.

One of the most annoying things about Harris' recollections is the lack of personal details, particularly those relating to his civilian life, therefore we do not know if he ever married and had a family. Over 150 years have passed since he told his story to Henry Curling, yet only now has he been positively identified as *Benjamin* Harris, his Christian name being a detail omitted from his *Recollections* by both himself and his first editor.

Harris' disinterest in the personal aspects of his life has made it very difficult to discover where he lived after 1814, or where and when he died, although the fact that he was awarded the Military General Service Medal suggests that he was alive in 1848 when they were issued. Had he returned to his home parish of Stalbridge in Dorset, such information would have been comparatively easy to trace. This did not happen, although he may have gone there occasionally to visit his brother. Frederick was a local carpenter, and during the latter part of his life (until 1859 at least), he was also a local publican. As Henry Curling discovered Benjamin working in London, and evidence in the text suggests that he was living in the city soon after his discharge - he met Robert Liston in Sloane Street, Chelsea in about 1818 - it would appear that he preferred to live and work in cosmopolitan London than return to rural Dorset.

At the time Henry Curling interviewed him, Harris was a shoemaker in Richmond Street, Soho. That was in about 1835. The London Commercial Directory for 1836 reveals that on the south side of Richmond Street - at No.8 - were the premises of a boot-maker called Jonathan Williamson. Was Harris working for him? Richmond Street linked Rupert Street with Princes Street (now Wardour Street), but it no longer exists under that name, having been incorporated into what we now know as Shaftesbury Avenue.

It is possible that, for a time, Harris ran his own shop in London because, on no less that three occasions between 1835 and 1838, Robson's Commercial Directory records the presence at 15 Queen Street, Golden Square, of Benj. Harris, boot-maker. However, a search for his name in other local records has not proved fruitful.

Harris regarded his period of military service as the most important phase of his life, so let us leave him with the last word, as he sits thinking and talking about his experiences in the shop in Richmond Street:

I remember a great many of the leaders and heroes of the wars of my time. Alas, of late they have been cleared off pretty handsomely! A few years more and the world will be without another living remembrancer of either them or their deeds. The ranks are getting thin, too, amongst those who, like myself, were the tools with which the great men of former days won their renown. I don't know a single living man now who was a comrade during the time I served.

Let me here bear testimony to the courage and endurance of that army under trials and hardships which few armies, in any age, can have endured. I have seen officers and men hobbling forwards, with ragged backs, without even shoes or stockings on their bleeding feet, and with tears in their eyes from the misery of long miles and empty stomachs (and it took a lot to bring a tear into the eye of a Rifleman of the Peninsula). Youths not long removed from their parents' home and care, officers and men, bore hardships and privations which, in our own more peaceful days, we have little conception of. Yet these same men, though faint and weary with toil, would brighten up in a moment when the word ran amongst us that the enemy were at hand.

The field of death and slaughter, the march, the bivouac, and the retreat, are not bad places in which to judge men. Having had the opportunity of doing so, I would say that the British are amongst the most splendid soldiers in the world. Give them fair play, and they are unconquerable.

I enjoyed life more whilst on active service that I have ever done since, and I look back upon my time spent in the fields of the Peninsula as the only part worthy of remembrance. As I sit at work in my shop in Richmond Street, Soho, scenes long passed come back upon my mind as if they had taken place but yesterday. I remember the appearance of some of the regiments engaged. And I remember too my comrades, long mouldered to dust, once again performing the acts of heroes.

NOTES

CHAPTER 1: *Shepherd and Recruit, 1781-1806*

1. 1802 in the 1848 edition.

2. The Militia Act of 1802 required that 51,500 men be raised nationally by ballot for an army of reserve. In 1803 another Act allowed for the enrolment of a further 25,000. The Office of the Royal Army of Reserve was responsible for carrying out these requirements. Harris' ballot paper has survived and is at the County Record Office in Dorchester. On it he is described as a cordwainer (shoemaker), who was enrolled on 13 August 1803 for a bounty of £11, which he received in October the same year. He 'signed' for the money by making his mark, thereby revealing his illiteracy.

3. Those enrolled with Harris included servants John Hatcher and James Gallop, painter Thomas Sanders, and Samuel Jenkins. Two men from the same area, balloted a year later, avoided service by paying the bounty to two substitutes, as they were allowed to do.

4. There is every likelihood that the man shot that day was Stephen Carroll of the 70th Regiment, who deserted at Chatham Barracks on 26 November 1802. It was his third desertion from the 70th since enlisting in May 1802. On the last occasion, he remained at large for a year, until brought back by a party on 1 October 1803. He was court-martialled at Sandgate on 27 October 1803. Most soldiers of the period who were found guilty of desertion were either flogged, transported as felons for seven or fourteen years, or banished (ie sentenced to serve in His Majesty's army overseas for the rest of their lives), although a petition in their favour, made by a senior officer, could mitigate the severity of the punishment. Carroll was unlucky: he was sentenced to be shot. No-one spoke up for him, and George III regretfully confirmed the sentence as a warning to

others. On 26 November 1803, the Judge-Advocate General wrote to Sir David Dundas, the officer in command of the forces in the southern district, requiring him to carry out the sentence as he thought proper, but recommending that it be made as public as possible, 'and that the same be conducted with the utmost solemnity'.

5. Lieutenant-General John Whitelocke, 1757-1833.

CHAPTER 2: *Danish Expedition, 1807*

1. Jonathan Leach, *Rough Sketches of the Life of an Old Soldier*, 1831; William Surtees, *Twenty-Five Years in the Rifle Brigade*, 1833; and William Green, *Travels and Adventures*, 1857. The original journals and memoirs of William Cox (1781-1857), and his brother John Cox (who joined the 95th in 1808), are held at the National Library of Ireland, with some extracts available on microfilm at the National Army Museum in Chelsea. Both are quoted by Willoughby Verner in his *History and Campaigns of the Rifle Brigade*, 1919.

2. The rockets had been invented by Sir William Congreve. They are not mentioned by Leach, Surtees or Green as having been used at Copenhagen.

3. Leach [Leech in previous editions], the author of *Rough Sketches*.

4. The King's German Legion had been formed by officers who fled Hanover when Napoleon took control of it in 1803. In 1807, most of the officers were German, but the rank and file included men of almost any nationality prepared to fight the French.

5. *Adventures in the Rifle Brigade*, 1830, and *Random Shots from a Rifleman*, 1835.

6. George Elder (Eleder in previous editions).

7. A Captain Dickenson fell at Montevideo at the head of a storming party.

CHAPTER 3: *Obidos and Roliça, August 1808*

1. The men's rations were one pound of biscuits and one pound of meat a day, and wine if the meat was salty. Their wives were allotted half-rations, but no wine.

2. Costello was on an equally long and harassing march in Portugal in similar conditions in July 1809. He described what each Rifleman - and these were the lightest troops - then had to carry: *"Knapsack and straps, two shirts, two pair of stockings, one pair of shoes, ditto soles and heels, three brushes, box of blacking, razor, soap-box and strap, and also at the time an extra pair of trousers; a mess-tin, centre-tin and lid, haversack and canteen, greatcoat and blanket, a powder-flask filled, a ball bag containing thirty loose balls, a small wooden mallet used to hammer the ball into the muzzle of our rifles; belt and pouch, the latter containing fifty rounds of ammunition, sword-belt and rifle, besides other odds and ends that at all times are required for a service-soldier. Each squad had also to carry four bill-hooks that weighed six pounds each, so that every other day each man had to carry it; thus [we were] equipped with from seventy to eighty pounds weight; [and] this, too, in the melting months of July"*.

3. Harris' discharge papers at the Public Record Office give his height as 5'5". He is further described as having black hair, grey eyes, and a dark complexion. In August 1808 he was 27 years old.

4. Rowland Hill, 1772-1842.

5. The bugle was used to signal movements to the Riflemen of the 95th. 'Fire and Retire' was the instruction to fall back.

6. There were two Pontons in the 95th, James and William. According to the regimental casualty returns, it was William Ponton - who with Harris had joined the 95th from the 66th Regiment in August 1806 - who was killed at Roliça, not James as stated in previous editions.

7. Cochan in previous editions.

8. John Simmons (Symmonds in previous editions), who joined in Ireland from the Wexford Militia on 12 September 1806.

9. He may have been a victim of local peasants, dying at the hands of the vengeful Portuguese in a manner described by William Lawrence of the 40th Regiment in his *Autobiography*: "*I came across one barbarous act where a ring of straw had been laid around a wounded Frenchman and set on fire. The man tried to crawl out but was forced back with a pitchfork. We fired at the Portuguese and made them fly, but the poor man's hair, fingers, and face were already fearfully burnt. He implored us not to leave him but we had to. No doubt the Portuguese returned and killed him*".

10. Leach: "*We bivouacked this night on the plains beyond the mountainous position from which the enemy had been expelled*".

11. With only six wives to every 100 soldiers allowed on campaign, most widows remained without husbands for only a short time.

CHAPTER 4: *Vimeiro, August 1808*

1. Charles Napier (1782-1853).

2. The name given in previous editions is Henry Jessop, but the records of the 95th reveal that the man who died was Joseph Jessop.

3. It had been five years!

4. Corporal John Murphy, from Dublin, was indeed killed at Vimeiro.

5. There were two Gillespies in the 2nd battalion - Corporal John and Private James. James is recorded as having been promoted to corporal a month after Vimeiro, so was it John who was wounded?

6. William Brotherwood is mentioned in the memoirs of Kincaid and Costello who were with the regiment when he was killed; Harris was not. Costello says that Lt.

Hopwood and Sgt. Brotherwood were killed on 9 December 1813 at a chateau called Arcangues near St. Jean de Luz as the French drove in the English pickets. George Simmons of the 95th said: *"A ball passed through both their heads, happening to be standing a little behind one another."* (Verner)

Kincaid: *"An officer of ours, Mr. Hopwood, and one of our sergeants, had been killed in the field opposite, within twenty yards of where the enemy's skirmishers were. We were very anxious to get possession of their bodies, but had not force enough to effect it. Several French soldiers came through the hedge at different times with the intention, as we thought, of plundering, but our men shot every one who attempted to go near them, until towards evening, when a French officer approached, waving a white handkerchief and pointing to some of his men who were following him with shovels. Seeing that his intention was to bury them, we instantly ceased firing; nor did we renew it again that night."*

Costello: *"Next day the enemy retreated within their works, upon which we took possession of our former ground and found the bodies of Lt. Hopwood and poor Brotherwood, both of which had been stripped, and covered partially with a little loose earth."*

7. Christopher Hibbert, in the 1970 edition of the *Recollections*, identified it as the King's German Legion, 2nd Light Battalion.

8. Leach said that when he and the other pickets joined their brigade on the left of the 97th, the business was beginning to assume a serious aspect: *"Some heavy masses of infantry, preceded by a swarm of light troops, were advancing with great resolution, and with loud cries of 'Vive l'Empereur! En avant' etc. against the hill on which our brigade was posted. In spite of the deadly fire which several hundred riflemen kept upon them, they continued to press forward with great determination, until the old 50th regiment received them with a destructive volley, following it instantly with a most brilliant and decisive charge with the bayonet, which broke and sent back in utter dismay and confusion, and with great loss,*

this column, which a short time before was all confidence and exultation."

9. Leach: *"The French column... was assailed in its retreat by the 20th Light Dragoons, who dashed gallantly amongst the fugitives and, in the ardour of the moment, following them to a distance from any support, encountered a very superior body of French cavalry, which obliged the 20th to fall back with some loss. Lt.-Col. Taylor fell whilst gallantly leading on his regiment in this charge."*

10. There were three men by the name of Mullen in the 95th at this time - Anthony, Stewart and Carrin (or Orrin).

11. According to Verner, Travers died in 1834.

12. John Lowe [Low in previous editions] survived the wars against Napoleon and was discharged on 25 May 1816.

CHAPTER 5: *After the Battle of Vimeiro, August 1808*

1. This may have been Major Hill whom Leach said had been in charge of his picket on the morning of the battle. Leach believed he had been killed while retreating to their own lines.

2. Portugal and Spain were Britain's allies and therefore regiments of their troops, including cavalry, fought alongside the British in all the major engagements of the Peninsular War. However, the majority of the resistance to the invader took the form of guerrilla warfare, to which the French responded with equal ruthlessness. So many atrocities were committed by French troops against civilians, that the Portuguese and Spanish revenged themselves in kind on nearly all the French stragglers, wounded soldiers and prisoners who fell into their hands.

3. Dr Thomas Hughes Ridgeway, of the 95th.

4. A Hugh Doughter enlisted in Ireland from the Londonderry Militia on 10 September 1806, a month later than Harris. If this is the same man, then Harris' knowledge of his fate was not shared with his regimental

administrators because the casualty returns record that Doughter's name was transferred to the newly formed 3rd battalion on 25 May 1809, along with the names of men listed as missing in action. The last entry for him was on 25 January 1810 when he was designated as a POW.

CHAPTER 6: *Lisbon to Salamanca and Sahagun, September - December 1808*

1. The Portuguese and Spanish, being Catholics, regarded the Protestant English as heretics. The Irish soldiers, most of whom were fellow Catholics, were therefore more acceptable to them.

2. Beresford had led the expeditionary force which in 1806 briefly held ascendancy over the Spanish in Buenos Aires. He was soon to be given the task of reorganising the Portuguese army.

3. It was nearer 200 miles.

4. There were several privates by the name of Baker in the 2nd battalion at this time - two Johns, one Edward and one William.

5. I haven't got the foggiest idea what Harris means by this. Have you?

6. Green on Salamanca: *"It was a splendid city, containing many thousands of inhabitants, with large shops; wine and every other commodity [was] very cheap".*

7. William Cox on reaching Zamora: *"I don't know that I ever felt so tired. I could scarcely crawl to my billet... I could procure only by much entreaty a cup of chocolate about the size of an egg-cup."*

CHAPTER 7: *Sahagun, December 1808*

1. William Surtees gives an excellent description of the quarters Baird's reinforcements were billeted in when staying at Betanzos a month earlier: *"We were here, as in most of the towns we afterwards passed through, lodged*

in convents, the officers generally either being quartered on the inhabitants of the town, or lodged by the monks in their cells. On these occasions, the men occupied only the corridors, into which straw was generally put by the authorities of the place, the men lying as close as pigs in a sty, which indeed was necessary to keep each other warm. But these lodgings were not to be complained of, as clean straw and shelter overhead are, in that country, no contemptible quarters."

CHAPTER 8: *Retreat to Corunna, 24 - 31 December 1808*

1. Although the memoirs and journals of brothers William and John Cox of the 95th are quoted in the *History of the Rifle Brigade,* Verner did not always make it clear which brother he was quoting. In this book, where the full identity of the diarist *is* known, it is stated. Where there is doubt, the source is given as Cox or Lt. Cox.

2. General Comte Charles Lefebvre-Desnouëttes (1773-1822).

3. Lt. Cox: *"Three companies [of the] 95th and two companies [of the] 43rd took post on the heights in front of the Bridge of Benevente this afternoon so as to protect the engineers mining it. We burnt a post house and some buildings here to prevent the enemy obtaining wood for a temporary bridge. After dark a French patrol approached our post but rode off again upon being fired upon, discharging their carbines in return. At midnight we crossed the half-destroyed bridge, and an arch having been blown up soon after, we joined the Reserve of the army at Benevente. We lay in the streets until daybreak."*

4. According to Christopher Hibbert, in a footnote to the 1985 edition of Harris's *Recollections,* Lefebvre-Desnouëttes was originally captured by a trooper of the King's German Legion who, not realising the value of his prize, allowed the man from the 10th Hussars to lead him off the field.

5. Surtees also witnessed the charge of the English dragoons against the French cavalry which *"were part of Bonaparte's Imperial Guard, and the flower of his army,*

being fine-looking men, dressed in dark-green long coats, with high bear-skin caps, and moustaches which gave them a formidable appearance. It was said that Bonaparte was looking on at this affair, and witnessed the defeat of his hitherto invincible Old Guard. It is certain that he slept the night before at Villalpando, a place only four leagues distant from the field."

6. Dudley St. Leger Hill (1770-1851) was a lieutenant in the 95th.

7. Unless there were two men of that name, Patrick McLaughlan did not perish on the retreat, for he is mentioned several times afterwards in the regimental records. On 25 April 1809, he was transferred to the 1st battalion, in which he was promoted to corporal (25 May 1809), and then demoted back to private on 5 February 1810.

CHAPTER 9: *Retreat to Vigo, 1 - 2 January 1809*

1. With the first battalion was Rifleman William Green, who gives a good account of his experiences in the rear of Moore's retreating army. He relates how the French cavalry, in advance of the French army, teased Moore's rear guard 'from morn til night': *"Their cavalry had a rifleman mounted behind each dragoon; and when any good position, or bushes by the road side, gave them any advantage to give our men a few shots, those riflemen would dismount and get under cover of the bushes, so that we were obliged to do the same. Their dragoons, at the same time dismounting, lay their carbines on their saddles, [and] with their horses standing in front of them for a sort of defence, would give us a few shots as well. In this way we were often obliged to make a stand and drive them back."*

2. There is no evidence in the records, or cited in Verner's *History*, that any officer of the 95th died of exhaustion on the retreat

3. After 1 January, those on the road to Vigo were no longer in danger of attack by the French, but they did not know that at the time.

4. In the muster books of the 95th, Sitdown's name is given variously as Siddown and Siddon. On 25 January 1809 he is referred to as missing, and on 15 June as missing in Spain. Then on 15 May 1809, along with other soldiers who went missing during the retreat, his name was transferred to the newly formed 3rd battalion. The last entry was on 24 January 1810 when he was listed as a POW.

5. Craufurd was a temperamental man, and a strict disciplinarian. Some of his soldiers feared and loved him; others feared and hated him, officers included. In his journals, to which Verner had access, Captain Jonathan Leach is critical of Craufurd. Six months after the retreat, while at Abrantes in Portugal, Leach wrote: *"Brigadier Robert Craufurd (damn him) issued this day to the Light Brigade an immensity of the most <u>tyrannical</u> and <u>oppressive standing orders</u> that were ever compiled by a British officer."*

6. Benjamin Jagger and Daniel Howard. In the 1848 edition Howard's name was transcribed as Howans. Benjamin Jagger survived the retreat, was promoted to corporal on 13 November 1810, but died in France on 1 March 1814.

7. Surtees was also present, and suggested that the floggings took place on 2nd January: *"Our road this day lay over high and almost inaccessible mountains, deeply covered with snow."*

8. Daniel Howard survived the retreat. His name appears in musters for several months afterwards.

9. Incorrectly transcribed as Hamilton Wade in previous editions

10. There were two Armstrongs in the 2nd battalion, George and Richard. They survived the retreat to Corunna and went on the Walcheren expedition six months later where

they caught Walcheren fever, from which they both died, at Hythe, in the autumn of 1809.

11. Harris was recounting his story in about 1835. I wonder what the 'late events' were that he is alluding to?

CHAPTER 10: *Recollections of the Retreat*

1. Philip Medley joined on 29 February 1808. Riflemen were required to be at least 5ft 2ins tall.

2. A later campaign in Spain, in the area of Cadiz, culminated in a battle at Barrossa in March 1811. It was not until a year later, on 30 October 1812, that Medley was reported as missing in Spain.

3. Thomas Higgins in previous editions.

4. Terence Higgins joined from the Cardiganshire Militia on 15 January 1808. The Casualty Returns list him as missing on 25 Jan. 1809, and on 25 May, like many other missing men, his name was placed on the roll of the newly-formed 3rd battalion.

5. Mrs McGuire's husband was probably William McGuire, a private in the 2nd battalion. After the retreat, he was promoted to corporal, then to sergeant, and then to Bugle Major. His son may have flourished but McGuire did not, dying at Hythe on 15 July 1811.

6. William Green of the 1st battalion, recorded that the captains were mounted, but that the lieutenants had to walk: *"I have seen some of them move on fast asleep until they have jostled on some of the men, and been thus awakened."*

7. According to Green, those in the 1st battalion who were retreating towards Corunna were ordered by their colonel to throw away their knapsacks but to retain their greatcoats, or their blankets, whichever they chose. However, they still had to carry *"fifty rounds of ball cartridge, thirty loose balls in our waist belt, and a flask, and a horn of powder, and rifle and sword, the two weighing 14 pounds. These were plenty for us to carry*

with empty bellies, and the enemy close at our heels, thirsting for our blood."

8. William Lawrence of the 40th Regiment was at the siege of Montevideo in February 1807. In his autobiography he recalls that when *"we reached the gunwharf, we found some twenty or thirty negroes chained to the guns. We spared them and later found them useful for burying the dead."* It would appear that Lt. Hill then found one of them equally useful as a servant.

9. There does not appear to have been a Lt. Keppel in the 2nd battalion of 95th, but there were two Beddells, Lt. Walter De'ath Beddell, and Ensign W. A. Beddell, although neither was reported as having died of fatigue on the retreat.

10. At this stage in the retreat, no soldier would have had either the inclination or the strength to carry an officer through a steam, and I therefore believe it happened earlier. It may, in fact, be another version of an incident recorded by Surtees as happening before the retreat, on the night of 23rd December, when the troops were advancing on the French from Sahagun. There were small brooks in the road and an officer of the 95th, who was unwell, walked round. Craufurd - Surtees does not name him, but it is obvious from his description that it was indeed the General - saw him and, in a great rage, forced the officer to go back, making him go through the brook again and again.

11. Whatever it was that Craufurd said, Harris did not hear it personally because after the Corunna campaign, he never again returned to Spain with his regiment.

CHAPTER 11: *Retreat to Vigo, 2 January - February 1809*

1. The regimental casualty returns bear this out. They record that James Brooks, formerly a Derry weaver, who was promoted to corporal soon after the Corunna campaign, died of his wounds in France on 26 March 1814

2.   William Cox?

3.   A Joseph Bell was in Leach's company with Harris during the early part of 1809. He was promoted to corporal in 1814 and to sergeant in 1815.

4.   Surtees says that the *Alfred* reached Spithead on 31 January, and that he landed on 1 February 1809. This was the same day that the *George and Mary* anchored off Portsmouth with Lt. Cox (and possibly Harris) aboard.

5.   Sir John Moore's army, which had retreated to Corunna, was there obliged to fight a battle with the pursuing French before embarking for England. Moore was killed.

6.   John, Michael and Peter Hart were in the same company as Harris. Six months after the retreat, they were sent on an expedition to the islands of the Scheldt river in the Netherlands, where fever quickly spread among the troops. Many of the 95th fell victim to it, including the Hart brothers. All three appear to have survived, their names appearing regularly in the muster books as late as December 1813. Michael was well enough to be promoted to Corporal on 25 December 1809. Similar evidence reveals that Peter and John Hart went up and down the rungs of promotion at a dizzying rate! Between 1805 and 1814, John Hart was demoted to private from the rank of corporal or sergeant no less than four times! The fact that the three of them appear to have survived the Peninsular War may be accounted for by the fact that they, like other survivors of Walcheren fever, were no longer fit for active service in the Peninsular, and therefore fulfilled military duties at home only.

7.   Was Mrs Pullen one of the group of women whose fate on the retreat was recorded by Rifleman William Green? He says *'we had seven or eight women belonging to the regiment. There were no baggage waggons on which they could ride, and some of them fell into the hands of the enemy who, after using them as they pleased, gave them some food, and sent them to us!'*

8.   Pullen died of Walcheren fever at Hythe on 20 October 1809.

CHAPTER 12: *Recruiting and Recruits, Spring 1809*

1. Lt. N. Pratt. Costello records that, near Almeida in 1810, Pratt was wounded in the neck, where the ball lodged. He later had a coughing fit, which caused it to sever the carotid artery. He bled to death and was buried at Coimbra.

2. John Lee's name first appears in the muster for the quarter 25 April - 24 June 1809. He was transferred to the 3rd battalion on 25 June 1809.

3. According to Verner, quoting Kincaid, the recruiting parties swept through quiet English country villages, rousing the sleeping inhabitants with the brazen notes of their bugles and shouting, *'Hurrah for the first in the field and the last out of it, the bloody fighting Ninety-fifth!'*

4. Mistakenly referred to as Shoreham Cliff in previous editions.

5. Thomas Deaman (Demon in previous editions) was made a sergeant in the 3rd battalion, and was stationed at Hythe throughout most of 1809.

CHAPTER 13: *The Walcheren Expedition, July - September 1809*

1. John Kincaid was also with the 95th. He had joined the 2nd battalion at Hythe Barracks in the spring of 1809. The Walcheren expedition was his first campaign with the regiment.

2. On 11 August, within two days of disembarkation, Major-General Stewart commented ominously on the unhealthiness of the island, and on the presence of agues in his men. There were: *'innumerable canals and ditches overgrown with weeds... the water of which is stagnant... Agues [of the] worst sort everywhere prevail. If we remain here another month in this part of the world, we are given to expect that one third of our Army will speedily become non-effective... At a gentleman's house at Graven Polder, I learned that of seventy French Hussars*

who were there quartered last year, thirty only were fit for duty in the course of six weeks halting there, and that a large proportion died."

3. On 27 August, Stewart reported that the 95th on South Beveland were falling sick at a rate of twenty a day. The doctors were puzzled by the cause of the illness, but in his *Adventures*, John Kincaid unwittingly gives modern readers a clue to its origins and identity. He too was on South Beveland *"where we remained about three weeks, playing at soldiers, smoking mynheer's long clay pipes, and drinking his vrow's butter-milk, for which I paid liberally with my precious blood to their infernal mosquitoes; not to mention that I had all the extra valour shaken out of me by a horrible ague, which commenced a campaign on my carcass."*

4. Nathan Booley?

5. They arrived at Deal about 16 September. Kincaid: *"One month saw us embark a thousand men at Deal, in the highest health, and spirits, and the next month saw us land, at the same place, with about seven hundred men carried to hospital, or staggering under disease."*

6. The muster roll for the period 16-25 September 1809 reveals that Major Norcott, 3 captains, 9 subalterns, 16 sergeants, 23 corporals, and 382 rifleman were sick. Twelve men died in the same period. Casualties as a consequence of enemy action were minimal.

7. In his *Adventures*, Kincaid says little about the Walcheren expedition and the effect of the fever upon him other than that it *"compelled me to retire upon Scotland, for the aid of my native air, by virtue of which it was ultimately routed. I shall not carry my first chapter beyond my first campaign, as I am anxious that my reader should not expend more than his first breath upon an event which cost too many their last."*

CHAPTER 14: *Invalid, 1810-1813*

1. Kincaid was one of the few men who returned successfully to active duty despite experiencing recurring

bouts of the fever. He not only fought throughout the rest of the Peninsular War, but survived the battle of Waterloo. In his *Random Shots from a Rifleman* (1835) he says: *"I cannot shake off that celebrated Walcheren fever without mentioning what may or may not be a peculiarity of it - that a brother-officer and I experienced a return of it within a day of each other, after a lapse of five years, and again, within a week, after the lapse of the following three years."*

2. As Harris was born in Portsea (as stated on his discharge papers), it is reasonable to assume that the family connection with the area was long-standing. This uncle was probably a Randell because the Stalbridge parish records reveal that his mother had at least three brothers, whereas his father appears to have had none.

3. Lt. Walter De'ath Beddell? In previous editions the name is transcribed as Bardell.

4. Henry William Paget (1768-1854), first Marquess of Anglesey (and a senior officer in Wellington's army) who in 1782 had inherited a large estate in North Dorset (including land and a manor in the parish of Stalbridge) from the Walter family.

5. He had been 21 years of age!

6. The village at which the coach stopped must have been Henstridge, situated midway between Shaftesbury and Sherborne on what was then known as the great western road. Although Henstridge was in Somerset, it was part of Stalbridge Parish. Then, as now, it had an inn called the Virginia Ash. It was surely the landlord of the Virginia Ash who arranged for Harris to be carried home to Stalbridge?

7. Regimental records confirm that Harris was sick at Hilsea from December 1809 to March 1811. It was probably between March and June 1811 that he returned to his family in Dorset because between June and December 1811 he is certified as being sick at Sturminster by surgeon John Burns. Harris' father, Robert, was living with his second wife Ann. Also at

home would have been Benjamin's brother Frederick 27 (soon to marry), his half brother James 14, and his half sister Lucy 8. Harris himself was 29 years old.

8.   He was probably in Dorchester by December 1811 because that is when the muster lists record that he was in the regimental hospital of the 9th Dragoons.

9.   As a private soldier, Harris received 7 shillings a week, ie just over £18 a year. For his medical services the doctor had charged this man, whose disablement had been acquired in the service of his country, the equivalent of three years' gross pay. Had Harris not been an army handicraft, with savings of his own, he would never have been able to pay the bill.

10.   A William McPherson of the 2nd Battalion was promoted to corporal in October 1813.

CHAPTER 15: *Soldiers of the 95th*

1.   Service in the army overseas for the rest of his life.

2.   Is it possible that Harris confused him with James Cummins of the 52nd Regiment who, along with 11 other deserters (three from the 95th), was recaptured after the siege of Ciudad Rodrigo in January 1812 and sentenced to be shot? James Cummins was, I believe, the only one of the 12 to be reprieved.

3.   Shoreham Cliff in previous editions.

CHAPTER 16: *Veteran*

1.   Frederick Augustus, Duke of York (1763-1827), the second son of George III, who had been appointed Commander-in-Chief of the army in 1798.

APPENDIX

Since the publication of the hardback edition of *A Dorset Rifleman* in April 1995, I have obtained information which either expands on what we already know of Benjamin Harris' life and narrative, or amends it in some way. That information I am presenting here in this brief appendix.

The most important new facts are those unearthed by Jack Stratfull in the Chelsea Hospital registers at the Public Record Office in Kew, and at the Westminster City Library. His research was published in the Journal of the Orders and Medals Research Society, Spring 1995.

Mr Stratfull reveals that Harris' pension, which he forfeited in 1814, was eventually restored (9d a day), but not until 1st January 1856. On 16th September that same year, Harris entered the Poland Street Workhouse, Westminster. The records of the Workhouse have survived, and Mr Stratfull discovered several entries referring to Harris. They make sad reading because in one entry he is described as 'insane', and in another as 'believed insane'. Was he suffering from an age related mental disorder? Three times between 16th September and 9th December 1856, he discharged himself. On the first occasion it was noted that he was going to live with his son-in-law. By 15th May 1857 he was back, in distress. Benjamin Randall Harris died in the Poland Street Workhouse on 10th December 1858, aged 77. The stated cause of death was disease of the prostate.

More research is needed into the latter part of Harris' life. If he had a son-in-law, then he had a daughter, and if he had a daughter, then surely he had a wife. And if he had a wife, who was she, and where did they marry? Where did they live? The last question can be partly answered - last year a copy of the 1848 edition of Harris' *Recollections* was being offered for sale by Maggs. Inside the cover, Curling had noted that, since the printing of the book had commenced, Benjamin Harris had progressed from Richmond Street to 4 Upper James St, Golden Square.

Another unsolved mystery is the burial place of the riflemen who died in Hythe of Walcheren fever. I originally thought that St Leonard's Church in Hythe was a possibility, but a much more likely site is suggested by Willoughby Verner in a footnote to his *History of the Rifle Brigade*, published in 1912. Verner reports that in 1892, at Hythe Barracks, the regiment's Colonel Slade found a sandstone slab built into the wall of an old ball-alley. It was etched with the Bugle Horn Badge, and with the inscription: *'95th Regt, 2nd Batt, 1811'*. It also bore the name of *'Lt. Col. H. Wade'*:

"There is no record of how or when this slab was built into the wall, but Colonel Slade ascertained that the old St Nicholas' Church and churchyard occupied the site of the present barracks, and that although the church was removed some 200 years ago, the churchyard was used at the beginning of the last century for the burial of soldiers who died there. Since over 130 of the 2nd battalion died after the return of the battalion from Walcheren in the years 1809-1810, there are fair grounds for his suggestion that this stone was formerly placed in the old graveyard which lay immediately below the ball-alley."

Since April 1995, I have received several letters, the contents of which have been very helpful in curing my puzzlement over Harris' reference to 'dumps'. I have learned that a 'dump' was a roughly-cast leaden counter used in games. One of these games, called 'pitch in the hole', or 'chuck-farthing', was like tiddly-winks, but it was known more simply as 'playing at dumps'. The OED gives another definition, one which further aids our understanding of Harris' comment. It quotes a reference which states that dumps are *"pieces of lead cast by schoolboys in the shape of money"* (Grose, *A Classic Dictionary of the Vulgar Tongue*, 1785). In other words, a dump was also a forged coin, which is exactly what some of Harris' comrades had turned their metal buttons into!

In a note to Chapter 10, I refer to two officers by the name of Beddell, but there was only one. He was Walter De'ath Beddell who joined the 95th as a second lieutenant on 19th March 1807. He was promoted to lieutenant on 11th August 1808 and remained with the regiment until 23th November 1815.

In Chapter 4, Harris tells us that Rifleman Patrick Mahone was killed alongside Lt. Hopwood and Sgt. Brotherwood (at Arcangues in 1813), but that is not so. Mahone (Mahony/Mahoney) survived the Peninsular War. His name appears on a special 1st battalion pay list of September 1815 as a 'Waterloo man'.

I am very grateful to Jack Stratfull for allowing me to quote from his article about Rifleman Harris, and to David Miles and Ian Fletcher for the information they supplied in the same context. And thank you again Miriam Collard, J Cooper Harding and Robert Williams for your help in resolving my query over 'dumps'.

Eileen Hathaway
September 1996

BIBLIOGRAPHY

BOOKS

A - Z of REGENCY LONDON. Introduction by Paul Laxton. Harry, Margary, Lympne Castle, Kent, 1985.

ATKINSON, J A   *Naval, Military, and Other Costumes of Great Britain*, 1807.

BAKER, M   *Discovering the Westward Stage*. Shire Publications, 1972.

BOND, G   *The Grand Expedition: the British Invasion of Holland in 1809.* University of Georgia Press, 1979

COSTELLO, E   *Adventures of a Soldier; or Memoirs of Edward Costello, comprising narratives of Wellington's Campaigns in the Peninsula, etc.* Colbourn & Co, London, 1841. Second editon, 1852. Later published as *The Peninsular and Waterloo Campaigns*, ed. Anthony Brett-James, Longman, 1967.

GODDARD   *Military Costumes of Europe*, 1812.

GREEN, W   *A Brief Outline of the Travels and Adventures of William Green, Bugler, Rifle Brigade.* Coventry, 1857.
Later edited by J and D Teague as *Where Duty Calls Me: the Experiences of William Green in the Napoleonic Wars.* Synjon Books (18 Manor Way, Orpington, Kent BR5 1NW), 1975.

HARRIS, B   *Recollections of Rifleman Harris*, edited by Henry Curling. London, 1848.
Edition of 1929 published by Peter Davies. Editions of 1970 and 1985, edited by Christopher Hibbert and published by Leo Cooper 1970, and Century Publishing 1985.

KINCAID, J   *Adventures in the Rifle Brigade*. London, 1830.

KINCAID, J   *Random Shots from a Rifleman*. London, 1835.

Adventures in the Rifle Brigade published in a combined edition with an abridged version of *Random Shots from a Rifleman*, 1909. Facsimile of combined edition published by Richard Drew Publishing, Glasgow, 1981

LAWRENCE, W   *A Dorset Soldier: the Autobiography of Sergeant William Lawrence 1790-1869*, edited by Eileen Hathaway. Spellmount, 1993.

Previously edited by G N Bankes and published by Sampson, Marston & Low, 1886. Facsimile of 1886 edition published by Ken Trotman, Cambridge, 1987.

LEACH, J   *Rough Sketches of the Life of an Old Soldier*. London, 1831. Facsimile of 1831 edition published by Ken Trotman, Cambridge, 1986.

LONGFORD, E   *Wellington: the Years of the Sword*. Literary Guild, 1969.

OMAN, Sir C   *Wellington's Army*. Edward Arnold, 1912.

PAGE, F C G   *Following the Drum: Women in Wellington's Wars*. Andre Deutsch, 1986.

SURTEES, W   *Twenty-Five Years in the Rifle Brigade*, 1833.

Facsimile of 1833 edition published by F Muller Ltd, 1973.

SWAYNE, W S   *A History of Stalbridge*. St Mary's Church.

VERNER, W   *History and Campaigns of the Rifle Brigade*, Vols. 1 and 2: 1800-1813. John Bale & Sons, London, 1912.

ARCHIVES

County Record Office, Dorchester

Blandford Forum Militia Papers PE/BF/OV8/1, 1799-1811
Parish Registers for Stalbridge
Documents relating to the Marquess of Anglesey's Estate in
Dorset. D/ANG
Universal British Directories

National Army Museum

Military memoirs and journals of Major-General William Cox
and Major-General John Cox. On microfilm. (Originals in
the National Library of Ireland.)

Public Record Office, Kew

Muster and pay lists for 95th - WO12
Discharge papers for 95th, Rifle Brigade, and 8th Veteran
Battalion - WO97
Casualty Returns for 95th - WO25/2143 and WO25/1334
General and Regimental Court Martial papers and registers in
WO71, WO90, and WO92

Royal Green Jackets Museum, Winchester

Regimental History, Uniforms, Portraits, Medals, Posters, etc

Westminster City Library, Victoria

Parish Registers and Census Returns for St. Anne's, Soho and
St. James', Piccadilly.
Robson's Commercial, and other trade directories 1820 -
1845.

Winchester Public Record Office and Public Library

Hampshire Chronicle, 1806
International Genealogical Index

INDEX